RUTH FIELDING OF THE RED MILL

OR, JASPER PARLOE'S SECRET

I0670811

ALICE B. EMERSON

Ruth Fielding of the Red Mill

Alice B. Emerson

© 1st World Library, 2007
PO Box 2211
Fairfield, IA 52556
www.1stworldlibrary.com
First Edition

LCCN: 2007934108

Softcover ISBN: 978-1-4218-9609-0
Hardcover ISBN: 978-1-4218-9709-7
eBook ISBN: 978-1-4218-9509-3

Purchase *"Ruth Fielding of the Red Mill"*
as a traditional bound book at:
www.1stWorldLibrary.com/purchase.asp?ISBN=978-1-4218-9609-0

1st World Library Literary Society

Giving Back to the World

"If you want to work on the core problem, it's early school literacy."

- James Barksdale, former CEO of Netscape

"No skill is more crucial to the future of a child, or to a democratic and prosperous society, than literacy."

- Los Angeles Times

"Literacy... means far more than learning how to read and write... The aim is to transmit... knowledge and promote social participation."

- UNESCO

"Literacy is not a luxury, it is a right and a responsibility. If our world is to meet the challenges of the twenty-first century we must harness the energy and creativity of all our citizens."

- President Bill Clinton

"Parents should be encouraged to read to their children, and teachers should be equipped with all available techniques for teaching literacy, so the varying needs and capacities of individual kids can be taken into account."

- Hugh Mackay

CHAPTER I

THE RED FLAME IN THE NIGHT

The sound of the drumming wheels! It had roared in the ears of Ruth Fielding for hours as she sat on the comfortably upholstered seat in the last car of the afternoon Limited, the train whirling her from the West to the East, through the fertile valleys of Upper New York State.

This had been a very long journey for the girl, but Ruth knew that it would soon come to an end. Cheslow was not many miles ahead now; she had searched it out upon the railroad timetable, and upon the map printed on the back of the sheet; and as the stations flew by, she had spelled their names out with her quick eyes, until dusk had fallen and she could no longer see more than the signal lamps and switch targets as the train whirled her on.

But she still stared through the window. This last car of the train was fairly well filled, but she had been fortunate in having a seat all to herself; she was glad this was so, for a person in the seat with her might have discovered how hard it was for her to keep back the tears.

For Ruth Fielding was by no means one of the "crying kind," and she had forbidden herself the luxury of tears on this occasion.

"We had all that out weeks ago, you know we did!" she whispered, apostrophizing that inner self that really wanted to break the brave compact. "When we knew we had to leave dear old Darrowtown, and Miss True Pettis, and Patsy Hope, and—and 'all other perspiring friends,' to quote Amoskeag Lanfell's letter that she wrote home from Conference.

"No, Ruth Fielding! Uncle Jabez Potter may be the very nicest kind of an old dear. And to live in a mill—and one painted red, too! That ought to make up for a good many disappointments—"

Her soliloquy was interrupted by a light tap upon her shoulder. Ruth glanced around and up quickly. She saw standing beside her the tall old gentleman who had been sitting two seats behind on the other side of the aisle ever since the train left Buffalo.

He was a spare old gentleman, with a gaunt, eagle-beaked face, cleanly shaven but for a sweeping iron-gray mustache, his iron-gray hair waved over the collar of his black coat—a regular mane of hair which flowed out from under the brim of his well-brushed, soft-crowned hat. His face would have been very stern in its expression had it not been for the little twinkle in his bright, dark eyes.

"Why don't you do it?" he asked Ruth, softly.

"Why don't I do what, sir?" she responded, not without a little gulp, for that lump would rise in her throat.

"Why don't you cry?" questioned the strange old gentleman, still speaking softly and with that little twinkle in his eye.

Alice B. Emerson

"Because I am determined not to cry, sir," and now Ruth could call up a little smile, though perhaps the corners of her mouth trembled a bit.

The gentleman sat down beside her, although she had not invited him to do so. She was not at all afraid of him and, after all, perhaps she was glad to have him do it.

"Tell me all about it," he suggested, with such an air of confidence and interest that Ruth warmed more and more toward him.

But it was a little hard to begin. When he told her, however, that he was going to Cheslow, too—indeed, that that was his home—it was easier by far.

"I am Doctor Davison, my dear," he said. "If you are going to live in Cheslow you will hear all about Doctor Davison, and you would better know him at first-hand, to avoid mistakes," and his eyes twinkled more than ever, though his stern mouth never relaxed.

"I expect that my new home is some little way outside of Cheslow," Ruth said, timidly. "They call it the Red Mill."

The humorous light faded out of the dark, bright eyes of the gentleman. Yet even then his countenance did not impress her as being unkindly.

"Jabez Potter's mill," he said, thoughtfully.

"Yes, sir. That is my uncle's name."

"Your uncle?"

"My great uncle, to be exact," said Ruth. "He was mother's uncle."

"Then you," he said, speaking even more gently than before, "are little Mary Potter's daughter?"

"Mother was Mary Potter before she married papa," said Ruth, more easily now. "She died four years ago."

He nodded, looking away from her out of the window at the fast-darkening landscape which hurried by them.

"And poor papa died last winter. I had no claim upon the kind friends who helped me when he died," pursued Ruth, bravely. "They wrote to Uncle Jabez and he—he said I could come and live with him and Aunt Alvirah Boggs."

In a flash the twinkle came back into his eyes, and he nodded again.

"Ah, yes! Aunt Alviry," he said, giving the name its old-fashioned, homely pronunciation. "I had forgotten Aunt Alviry," and he seemed quite pleased to remember her.

"She keeps house for Uncle Jabez, I understand," Ruth continued. "But she isn't my aunt."

"She is everybody's Aunt Alviry, I think," said Doctor Davison, encouragingly.

For some reason this made Ruth feel better. He spoke as though she would love Aunt Alviry, and Ruth had left so many kind friends behind her in Darrowtown that she was glad to be assured that somebody in the new home where she was going would be kind, too.

Alice B. Emerson

Miss True Pettis had not shown her Uncle Jabez's letter and she had feared that perhaps her mother's uncle {whom she had never seen nor known much about) might not have written as kindly for his niece to come to the Red Mill as Miss True could have wished. But Miss True was poor; most of the Darrowtown friends had been poor people. Ruth had felt that she could not remain a burden on them.

Somehow she did not have to explain all this to Doctor Davison. He seemed to understand it when he nodded and his eyes twinkled so glowingly.

"Cheslow is a pleasant town. You will like it," he said, cheerfully. "The Red Mill is five miles out on the Lake Osago Road. It is a pretty country. It will be dark when you ride over it to-night; but you will like it when you see it by daylight."

He took it for granted that Uncle Jabez would come to the station to meet her with a carriage, and that comforted Ruth not a little.

"You will pass my house on that road," continued Doctor Davison. "But when you come to town you must not pass it."

"Sir?" she asked him, surprised.

"Not without stopping to see me," he explained, his eyes twinkling more than ever. And then he left her and went back to his seat.

But Ruth found, when he had gone, that the choke came back into her throat again and the sting of unshed tears to her eyes. But she would not let those same tears fall!

She stared out of the plate-glass window and saw that it was now quite dark. The whistle of the fast-flying locomotive shrieked its long-drawn warning, and a group of signal lights flashed past. Then she heard the loud ringing of a gong at a grade crossing. They must be nearing Cheslow now.

And then she saw that they were on a curve quite a sharp curve, for she saw the lights of the locomotive and the mail car far ahead upon the gleaming rails. They began to slow down, too, and the wheels wailed under the pressure of the brakes.

She could see the signal lights along the tracks ahead and then—with a start, for she knew what it meant—a sharp red flame appeared out of the darkness beyond the rushing engine pilot.

Danger! That is what that red light meant. The brakes clamped down upon the wheels again so suddenly that the easily-riding coach jarred through all its parts. The red eye was winked out instantly; but the long and heavy train came to an abrupt stop.

Alice B. Emerson

CHAPTER II

RENO

But the Limited had stopped so that Ruth could see along the length of the train. Lanterns winked and blinked in the dark as the trainmen carried them forward. Something had happened up front of more importance than an ordinary halt for permission to run in on the next block. Besides, the afternoon Limited was a train of the first-class and was supposed to have the right of way over all other trains. No signal should have stopped it here.

"How far are we from Cheslow, please?" she asked of the rear brakeman (whom she knew was called the flagman) as he came down the car with his lantern.

"Not above a mile, Miss," he replied.

His smile, and his way of speaking, encouraged her to ask:

"Can you tell me why we have stopped?"

"Something on the track, Miss. I have set out my signal lamp and am going forward to inquire."

Three or four of the male passengers followed him out of the car. Ruth saw that quite a number had disembarked from the cars ahead, that a goodly company was moving forward, and that there were ladies among the curious crowd. If it was perfectly safe for them to satisfy their curiosity, why not she? She arose and hurried out of the car, following the swinging lamp of the brakeman as he strode on.

Ruth ran a little, seeing well enough to pick her way over the ends of the ties, and arrived to find at least half a hundred people grouped on the track ahead of the locomotive pilot. The great, unblinking, white eye of the huge machine revealed the group clearly—and the object around which the curious passengers, as well as the train crew, had gathered.

It was a dog—a great, handsome, fawn-colored mastiff, sleek of coat and well fed, but muddied now along his flanks, evidently having waded through the mire of the wet meadow beside the tracks. He had come under, or through, a barbed wire fence, too, for there was a long scratch upon his shoulder and another raw cut upon his muzzle.

To his broad collar was fastened a red lamp. Nobody had taken it off, for both the train men and the passengers were excitedly discussing what his presence here might mean; and some of them seemed afraid of the great fellow.

But Ruth had been used to dogs, and this noble looking fellow had no terrors for her. He seemed so woebegone, his great brown eyes pleaded so earnestly, that she could only pity and fondle him.

"Look out, Miss; maybe he bites," warned the anxious conductor. "I wager this is some boy's trick to stop the train. And yet—"

Ruth bent down, still patting the dog's head, and turned the great silver plate on his collar so that she could read, in the light of the lanterns, that which was engraved upon it. She read the words aloud:

"'This is Reno, Tom Cameron's Dog.'"

"Cameron?" repeated some man behind her. "That Tom Cameron lives just outside of Cheslow. His father is the rich dry-goods merchant, Macy Cameron. What's his dog doing here?"

"And with a red light tied to his collar?" propounded somebody else.

"It's some boy's trick, I tell you," stormed the conductor. "I'll have to report this at headquarters."

Just then Ruth made a discovery. Wound about the collar was a bit of twisted cloth—a strip of linen—part of a white handkerchief. Her nimble fingers unwound it quickly and she spread out the soiled rag.

"Oh, see here!" she cried, in amazement as well as fear. "See! What can it mean? See what's drawn on this cloth—"

It was a single word—a word smeared across the rag in shaking, uneven letters:

"HELP!"

"By George!" exclaimed one of the brakemen. "The little girl's right. That spells 'Help!' plain enough."

"It—it is written in something red, sir," cried Ruth, her voice trembling. "See! It is blood!"

"I tell you we've wasted a lot of time here," declared the conductor. "I am sorry if anybody is hurt, but we cannot stop for him. Get back to the cars, please, gentlemen. Do you belong aboard?" he added, to Ruth. "Get aboard, if you do."

"Oh, sir! You will not leave the poor dog here?" Ruth asked.

"Not with that red lamp on his collar—no!" exclaimed the conductor. "He will be fooling some other engineer—"

He reached to disentangle the wire from the dog's collar; but Reno uttered a low growl.

"Plague take the dog!" ejaculated the conductor, stepping back hastily. "Whoever it is that's hurt, or wherever he is, we cannot send him help from here. We'll report the circumstance at the Cheslow Station. Put the dog in the baggage car. He can find the place where his master is hurt, from Cheslow as well as from here, it's likely."

"You try to make him follow you, Miss," added the conductor to Ruth. "He doesn't like me, it's plain."

"Come here, Reno!" Ruth commanded. "Come here, old fellow."

The big dog hesitated, stepped a yard or two after her, stopped, looked around and across the track toward the swamp meadow, and whined.

Ruth went back to him and put both arms about the noble fellow's neck. "Come, Reno," she said "Come with me. We will go to find your master by and by."

She started for the cars again, with one hand on the dog's neck. He trotted meekly beside her with head hanging. At the

Alice B. Emerson

open baggage-car door one of the brakemen lifted her in.

"Come, Reno! Come up, sir!" she said, and the great mastiff, crouching for an instant, sprang into the car.

Even before they were fairly aboard, the train started. They were late enough, indeed! But the engineer dared not speed up much for that last mile of the lap to Cheslow. There might be something ahead on the track."

"You get out at Cheslow; don't you Miss?" asked the conductor.

"Yes, sir," returned Ruth, sitting down with an air of possession upon her old-fashioned cowhide trunk that had already been put out by the door ready for discharging at the next station.

"And you were sitting in the last car. Have you a bag there?"

"Yes, sir, a small bag. That is all."

"I'll send it forward to you," he said, not unkindly, and bustled away.

And so Ruth Fielding was sitting on her own trunk, with her bag in her lap, and the great mastiff lying on the floor of the baggage car beside her, when the train slowed down and stopped beside the Cheslow platform. She had not expected to arrive just in this way at her journey's end.

CHAPTER III

WHAT HAS HAPPENED?

The baggage-car door was wheeled wide open again and the lamps on the platform shone in. There was the forward brakeman to "jump" her down from the high doorway, and Reno, with the little red light still hung to his collar, bounded after her.

The conductor bustled away to tell the station master about the dog with the red light, and of the word scrawled on the cloth which Ruth had found wound around his collar. Indeed, Ruth herself was very anxious and very much excited regarding this mystery; but she was anxious, too, about herself. Was Uncle Jabez here to meet her? Or had he sent somebody to take her to the Red Mill? He had been informed by Miss True Pettis the week before on which train to expect his niece.

Carrying her bag and followed dejectedly by the huge mastiff, Ruth started down the long platform. The conductor ran out of the station, signalled the train crew with his hand, and lanterns waved the length of the train. Panting, with its huge springs squeaking, the locomotive started the string of cars. Faster and faster the train moved, and before Ruth reached the pent-house roof of the little brick station, the tail-lights of the last car had passed her.

A short, bullet-headed old man, with close-cropped, whitish-yellow hair, atop of which was a boy's baseball cap, his face smoothly shaven and deeply lined, and the stain of tobacco at either corner of his mouth, was standing on the platform. He was not a nice looking old man at all, he was dressed in shabby and patched garments, and his little eyes seemed so sly that they were even trying to hide from each other on either side of a hawksbill nose.

He began to eye Ruth curiously as the girl approached, and she, seeing that he was the only person who gave her any attention, jumped to the conclusion that this was Uncle Jabez. The thought shocked her. She instinctively feared and disliked this queer looking old man. The lump in her throat that would not be swallowed almost choked her again, and she winked her eyes fast to keep from crying.

She would, in her fear and disappointment, have passed the old man by without speaking had he not stepped in front of her.

"Where d'ye wanter go, Miss?" he whined, looking at her still more sharply out of his narrow eyes. "Yeou be a stranger here, eh?"

"Yes, sir," admitted Ruth.

"Where are you goin'?" asked the man again, and Ruth had enough Yankee blood in her to answer the query by asking:

"Are you Mr. Jabez Potter?"

"Me Jabez Potter? Why, ef I was Jabe Potter I'd be owing myself money, that's what I'd be doin'. You warn't never lookin' for Jabe Potter?"

Much relieved, Ruth admitted the fact frankly. "He is my uncle, sir," she said. "I am going to live at the Red Mill."

The strange old man puckered up his lips into a whistle, and shook his head, eyeing her all the time so slily that Ruth was more and more thankful that he had not proven to be Uncle Jabez.

"Do you know Mr. Potter?" she asked, undecided what to do.

"Do I know Jabe Potter?" repeated the man. "Well, I don't know much good of him, I assure ye! I worked for him onct, I did. And I tell ye he owes me money yet. You ax him if he don't owe Jasper Parloe money—you jest ax him!"

He began to get excited and did not seem at all inclined to step out of Ruth's path. But just then somebody spoke to her and she turned to see the station master and two or three other men with him.

"This is the girl Mr. Mason spoke to me about, isn't it?" the railroad man asked. "The conductor of the express, I mean. He said the dog would mind you."

"He seems to like me," she replied, turning to the mastiff that had stood all this time close to her.

"That is Tom Cameron's dog all right," said one of the other men. "And that lantern is off his motorcycle, I bet anything! He went through town about dark on that contraption, and I shouldn't wonder if he's got a tumble."

Ruth showed the station master, whose name was Curtis, the bit of handkerchief with the appeal for help traced upon it.

Alice B. Emerson

"That is blood," she said. "You see it's blood, don't you? Can't somebody take Reno and hunt for him? He must be very badly hurt."

"Mason said he expected it was nothing but some fool joke of the boys. But it doesn't look like a joke to me," Mr. Curtis said, gravely. "Come, Parloe, you know that patch of woods well enough, over beyond the swamp and Hiram Jennings' big field. Isn't there a steep and rocky road down there, that shoots off the Osago Lake pike?"

"The Wilkins Corners road—yep," said the old man, snappishly.

"Then, can't you take the dog and see if you can find young Tom?"

"Who's going to pay me for it?" snarled Jasper Parloe. "I ain't got no love for them Camerons. This here Tom is as sassy a boy as there is in this county."

"But he may be seriously hurt," said Ruth, looking angrily at Jasper Parloe.

"'Tain't nothin' to me—no more than your goin' out ter live with Jabe Potter ain't nothin' to me," responded the old man, with an ugly grin.

"You're a pretty fellow, you are, Jasper!" exclaimed Mr. Curtis, and turned his back upon the fellow. "I can't leave the station now—Ah! here's Doctor Davison. He'll know what to do."

Doctor Davison came forward and put his hand upon Ruth's shoulder most kindly. "What is all this?" he asked. "And there is the mastiff. They tell me you are a dog tamer,

Miss Fielding."

He listened very closely to what Mr. Curtis had to say, and looked, too, at the smeared handkerchief.

"The dog can find him—no doubt of that. Come, boys, get some lanterns and we'll go right along to the Wilkins Corners road and search it." Then to Ruth he said: "You are a brave girl, sure enough."

But when the party was ready to start, half a dozen strong, with Parloe trailing on behind, and with lanterns and a stretcher, Reno would not budge. The man called him, but he looked up at Ruth and did not move from her side.

"I declare for't," exclaimed one man. "That girl will have to go with us, Doctor Davison. You see what the dog means to do."

Ruth spoke to the mastiff, commanded him to leave her and find "Tom." But although the dog looked at her intelligently enough, and barked his response—a deep, sudden, explosive bark—he refused to start without her.

"It's a long way for the girl," objected Doctor Davison. "Besides, she is waiting to meet her uncle."

"I am not tired," she told him, quickly. "Remember I've been sitting all the afternoon. And perhaps every minute is precious. We don't know how badly the dog's master may be hurt. I'll go. I'm sure I can keep up with you."

Reno seemed to understand her words perfectly, and uttered another short, sharp bark.

"Let us go, then," said Doctor Davison, hurriedly.

Alice B. Emerson

So the men picked up their lanterns and the stretcher again. They crossed the tracks and came to a street that soon became a country road. Cheslow did not spread itself very far in this direction. Doctor Davison explained to Ruth that the settlement had begun to grow in the parts beyond the railroad and that all this side of the tracks was considered the old part of the town.

The street lights were soon behind them and they depended entirely upon the lanterns the men carried. Ruth could see very little of the houses they passed; but at one spot—although it was on the other side of the road—there were two green lanterns, one on either side of an arched gate, and there seemed to be a rather large, but gloomy, house behind the hedge before which these lanterns burned.

"You will always know my house," Doctor Davison said, softly, and still retaining her hand, "by its green eyes."

So Ruth knew she had passed his home, to which he had so kindly invited her. And that made her think for a moment about Uncle Jabez and Aunt Alvirah. Would she find somebody waiting to take her to the Red Mill when she got back to the station?

CHAPTER IV

THE GATE OF THE GREEN EYES

It was a dark lane, beneath overhanging oaks, that met and intertwined their branches from either side—this was the Wilkins Corners road. And it was very steep and stony—up hill and down dale—with deep ruts in places and other spots where the Spring rains had washed out the gravel and sand and left exposed the very foundations of the world.

It seemed as though no bicyclist, or motor-cyclist would have chosen this road to travel after dark. Yet there was a narrow path at the side—just wide enough for Ruth and Doctor Davison to walk abreast, and Reno to trot by the girl's side which seemed pretty smooth.

"We don't want to go by the spot, Doctor," said one of the men walking ahead with the lights. "Don't the dog show no signs of looking for Tom?"

"Where's Tom, Reno? Where's Tom?" asked Ruth, earnestly, believing that the dog would recognize his master's name.

The mastiff raised his muzzle and barked sharply again, but trotted onward.

Alice B. Emerson

"He might have fallen down any of these gullies, and we'd miss him, it's so dark," observed the previous speaker.

"I don't believe the dog will miss the place," responded Doctor Davison.

Just then Reno leaped forward with a long-drawn whine. Ruth hurried with him, leaving the doctor to come on in the rear. Reno took the lead and the girl tried to keep pace with him.

It was not for many yards. Reno stopped at the brink of a steep bank beside the road. This bank fell away into the darkness, but through the trees, in the far distance, the girl could see several twinkling lights in a row. She knew that they were on the railroad, and that she was looking across the great swamp-meadow.

"Hullo!" shouted one man, loudly. "Something down there, old fellow?"

Reno answered with a short bark and began to scramble down the rough bank.

"Here's where somebody has gone down ahead of him," cried another of the searchers, holding his own lantern close to the ground. "See how the bank's all torn up? Bet his wheel hit that stone yonder in the dusk and threw him, wheel and all, into this gulley."

"Wait here, child," ordered Doctor Davison, quickly. "If he is in bad shape, boys, call me and I'll come down. Lift him carefully—"

"He's here, sir!" cried the first man to descend.

And then Reno lifted up his voice in a mournful howl.

"Oh, dear! oh, dear!" murmured Ruth. "I am afraid he is badly hurt."

"Come, come!" returned Doctor Davison. "Be a brave girl now. If he is badly hurt he'll need us both to keep our wits about us, you know."

"Ye needn't fret none, leetle gal," said Jasper Parloe's voice, behind her. "Ye couldn't kill that there Cameron boy, I tell ye! He is as sassy a young'un as there is in this county."

Doctor Davison turned as though to say something sharp to the mean old man; but just then the men below shouted up to him:

"He's hit his head and his arm's twisted under him, Doctor. He isn't conscious, but doesn't seem much hurt otherwise."

"Can you bring him up?" queried the physician.

"That's what we mean to do," was the reply.

Ruth waited beside the old doctor, not without some apprehension. How would this Tom Cameron look? What kind of a boy was he? According to Jasper Parloe he was a very bad boy, indeed. She had heard that he was the son of a rich man. While the men were bringing the senseless body up the steep bank her mind ran riot with the possibilities that lay in store for her because of this accident to the dry-goods merchant's son.

And now the bearers were at the top of the bank, and she could see the limp form borne by them—a man holding the body under the arms and another by his feet. But, altogether, it looked really as though they carried a limp sack between them.

"Fust time I ever see that boy still," murmured Jasper Parloe.

"Cracky! He's pale; ain't he?" said another man.

Doctor Davison dropped on one knee beside the body as they laid it down. The lanterns were drawn together that their combined light might illuminate the spot. Ruth saw that the figure was that of a youth not much older than herself—lean, long limbed, well dressed, and with a face that, had it not been so pale, she would have thought very nice looking indeed.

"Poor lad!" Ruth heard the physician murmur. "He has had a hard fall—and that's a nasty knock on his head."

The wound was upon the side of his head above the left ear and was now all clotted with blood. It was from this wound, in some moment of consciousness, that he had traced the word "Help" on his torn handkerchief, and fastened the latter, with the lamp of his motorcycle, to the dog's collar.

Here was the machine, bent and twisted enough, brought up the bank by two of the men.

"Dunno what you can do for the boy, Doctor," said one of them; "but it looks to me as though this contraption warn't scurcely wuth savin'."

"Oh, we'll bring the boy around all right," said Doctor Davison, who had felt Tom Cameron's pulse and now rose quickly. "Lift him carefully upon the stretcher. We will get him into bed before I do a thing to him. He's best as he is while we are moving him."

"It'll be a mighty long way to his house," grumbled one of the men.

"I believe yeou!" rejoined Jasper Parloe. "Three miles beyond Jabe Potter's mill."

"Pshaw!" exclaimed Doctor Davison, in his soft voice. "You know we'll not take him so far. My house is near enough. Surely you can carry him there."

"If you say the word, Doctor," said the fellow, more cheerfully, while old Parloe grunted.

They were more than half an hour in getting to the turn in the main road where she could observe the two green lights before the doctor's house. There the men put the stretcher down for a moment. Jasper Parloe grumblingly took his turn at carrying one end.

"I never did see the use of boys, noway," he growled. "They's only an aggravation and vexation of speret. And this here one is the aggravatingest and vexationingest of any I ever see."

"Don't be too hard on the boy, Jasper," said Doctor Davison, passing on ahead, so as to reach his house first.

Ruth remained behind, for the old gentleman walked too fast for her. Before the men picked up the stretcher again there was a movement and a murmur from the injured boy.

"Hullo!" said one of the men. "He's a-talkin', ain't he?"

"Jest mutterin'," said Parloe, who was at Tom's head. "'Tain't nothi

But Ruth heard the murmur of the unconscious boy, and the words startled her. They were:

"It was Jabe Potter—he did it! It was Jabe Potter—he did it!"

What did they mean? Or, was there no meaning at all to the muttering of the wounded boy? Ruth saw that Parloe was looking at her in his sly and disagreeable way, and she knew that he, too, had heard the words.

"It was Jabe Potter—he did it!" Was it an accusation referring to the boy's present plight? And how could her Uncle Jabez—the relative she had not as yet seen—be the cause of Tom Cameron's injury? The spot where the boy was hurt must have been five miles from the Red Mill, and not even on the Osago Lake turnpike, on which highway she had been given to understand the Red Mill stood.

Not many moments more and the little procession was at the gateway, on either side of which burned the two green lamps.

Jasper Parloe, who had been relieved, shuffled off into the darkness. Reno after one pleading look into the face of the hesitating Ruth, followed the stretcher on which his master lay, in at the gate.

And Ruth Fielding, beginning again to feel most embarrassed and forsaken, was left alone where the two green eyes winked in the warm, moist darkness of the Spring night.

CHAPTER V

THE GIRL IN THE AUTOMOBILE

The men who had gone in with the unconscious boy and the stretcher hung about the doctor's door, which was some yards from the gateway. Everybody seemed to have forgotten the girl, a stranger in Cheslow, and for the first day of her life away from kind and indulgent friends.

It was only ten minutes walk to the railroad station, and Ruth remembered that it was a straight road. She arrived in the waiting room safely enough. Sam Curtis, the station master, descried her immediately and came out of his office with her bag.

"Well, and what happened? Is that boy really hurt?" he asked.

"He has a broken arm and his head is cut. I do not know how seriously, for Doctor Davison had not finished examining him when I—I came away," she replied, bravely enough, and hiding the fact that she had been overlooked.

"They took him to the doctor's house, did they?" asked Sam.

"Yes, sir," said Ruth. "But—"

Alice B. Emerson

"Mr. Curtis, has there been anybody here for me?"

"For you, Miss?" the station master returned, somewhat surprised it seemed.

"Yes, sir. Anybody from Red Mill?"

Curtis smote one fist into his other palm, exclaiming:

"You don't mean to say that you was what Jabe Potter was after?"

"Mr. Jabez Potter, who keeps the Red Mill, is my uncle," Ruth observed, with dignity.

"My goodness gracious me, Miss! He was here long before your train was due. He's kind of short in his speech, Miss. And he asked me if there was anything here for him, and I told him no. And he stumped out again without another word. Why, I thought he was looking for an express package, or freight. Never had an idea he was expectin' a niece!"

Ruth still looked at him earnestly. The man did not suspect, by her appearance, how hard a time she was having to keep the tears from overrunning those calm, gray eyes.

"And you expected to go out to the Red Mill to-night, Miss?" he continued. "They're country folk out there and they'd all be abed before you could get there, even if you took a carriage."

"I don't know that I have enough to pay for carriage hire," Ruth said, softly. "Is—is there any place I can stop over night in the village? Then I can walk out in the morning."

"Why—there's a hotel. But a young girl like you—You'll

excuse me, Miss. You're young to be traveling alone."

"Perhaps I haven't money enough to pay for a lodging there?" suggested Ruth. "I have a dollar. It was given me to spend as I liked on the way. But Miss True gave me such a big box of luncheon that I did not want anything."

"A dollar wouldn't go far at the Brick Hotel," murmured the station agent. He still stared at her, stroking his lean, shaven jaw. Finally he burst out with: "I tell you! We'll go home and see what my wife says."

At the moment the station began to jar with the thunder of a coming train and Ruth could not make herself heard in reply to his proposal. Besides, Sam Curtis hurried out on the platform. Nor was Ruth ready to assert her independence and refuse any kind of help the station master might offer. So she sat down patiently and waited for him.

There were one or two passengers only to disembark from this train and they went away from the station without even coming into the waiting room. Then Curtis came back, putting out the lights and locking his ticket office. The baggage room was already locked and Ruth's old trunk was in it.

"Come on now, girl—What's your name?" asked Curtis.

"Ruth Fielding."

"Just so! Well, it's only a step to our house and wife will have supper waiting. And there's nobody else there save Mercy."

Ruth was a little curious about "Mercy"—whether it referred to abounding grace, or was a person's name. But she asked

Alice B. Emerson

no questions as they came out of the railroad station and Sam Curtis locked the door.

They did not cross the tracks this time, but went into the new part of the town. Turning a corner very soon as they walked up what Curtis said was Market Street, they reached, on a narrow side street, a little, warm-looking cottage, from almost all the lower windows of which the lamplight shone cheerfully. There was a garden beside it, with a big grape arbor arranged like a summer-house with rustic chairs and a table. The light shining on the side porch revealed the arbor to Ruth's quick eyes.

When they stepped upon this porch Ruth heard a very shrill and not at all pleasant voice saying—very rapidly, and over and over again: "I don't want to! I don't want to! I don't want to!" It might have been a parrot, or some other ill-natured talking bird; only Ruth saw nothing of the feathered conversationalist when Sam opened the door and ushered her in.

"Here we are, wife!" he exclaimed, cheerfully. "And how's Mercy?"

The reiterated declaration had stopped instantly. A comely, kind-faced woman with snow-white hair, came forward. Ruth saw that she was some years younger than Curtis, and he was not yet forty. It was not Father Time that had powdered Mrs. Curtis' head so thickly.

"Mercy is—Why, who's this?" she asked espying Ruth. "One of the girls come in to see her?"

Instantly the same whining, shrill voice began:

"I don't want her to see me! They come to stare at me! I hate 'em all! All girls do is to run and jump and play tag and ring-around-a-rosy and run errands, and dance! I hate 'em!"

This was said very, very fast—almost chattered; and it sounded so ill-natured, so impatient, so altogether mean and hateful, that Ruth fell back a step, almost afraid to enter the pleasant room. But then she saw the white-haired lady's face, and it was so grieved, yet looked such a warm welcome to her, that she took heart and stepped farther in, so that Sam Curtis could shut the door,

The father appeared to pay no attention to the fault-finding, shrill declamation of the unhappy voice. He said, in explanation, to his wife:

"This is Ruth Fielding. She has come a long. way by train to-day, expecting to meet her uncle, old Jabe Potter of the Red Mill. And you know how funny Jabe is, wife? He came before the train, and did not wait, but drove right away with his mules and so there was nobody here to meet Ruthie. She's marooned here till the morning, you see."

"Then she shall stay with us to-night," declared Mrs. Curtis, quickly.

"I don't want her to stay here to-night!" ejaculated the same shrill voice.

Mr. and Mrs. Curtis paid no attention to what was said by this mysterious third party. Ruth, coming farther into the room, found that it was large and pleasant. There was a comfortable look about it all. The supper table was set and the door was opened into the warm kitchen, from which delicious odors of tea and toast with some warm dish of meat, were wafted in. But the shrill and complaining voice had not come from the next room.

In the other corner beside the stove, yet not too near it, stood a small canopy bed with the pretty chintz curtains drawn all about it. Beside it stood a wheel-chair such as Ruth knew was used by invalids who could not walk. It was a tiny chair, too, and it and the small bed went together. But of the occupant of either she saw not a sign.

"Supper will be ready just as soon as our guest has a chance to remove the traces of travel, Sam," said Mrs. Curtis, briskly. "Come with me, Ruth."

When they returned from the pleasant little bed-chamber which the good-hearted lady told Ruth was to be her own for that night, they heard voices in the sitting room—the voice of Mr. Curtis and the querulous one. But it was not so sharp and strained as it seemed before. However, on opening the door, Mr. Curtis was revealed sitting alone and there was no sign of the owner of the sharp voice, which Ruth supposed must belong to the invalid.

"Mercy has had her supper; hasn't she, wife?" said the station master as he drew his chair to the table and motioned Ruth to the extra place Mrs. Curtis had set.

The woman nodded and went briskly about putting the supper on the table. While they ate Mr. Curtis told about Reno stopping the train, and of the search for and recovery of the injured Cameron boy. All the time Ruth, who sat sideways to the canopied bed, realized that the curtains at the foot were drawn apart just a crack and that two very bright, pin-point eyes were watching her. So interested did these eyes become as the story progressed, and Ruth answered questions, that more of Mercy Curtis' face was revealed—a sharp, worn little face, with a peaked chin and pale, thin cheeks.

Ruth was very tired when supper was ended and the kind Mrs. Curtis suggested that she go to bed and obtain a good night's rest if she was to walk to the Red Mill in the morning. But even when she bade her entertainers good-night she did not see the child in the canopy bed and she felt diffident about asking Mrs. Curtis about her. The young traveler slept soundly—almost from the moment her head touched the pillow. Yet her last thought was of Uncle Jabez. He had been in town some time before the train on which she arrived was due and had driven away from the station with his mules, Mr. Curtis said. Had he driven over that dark and dangerous road on which Tom Cameron met with his accident, and had he run down the injured boy, or forced him over the bank of the deep gully where they had found Tom lying unconscious?

"It was Jabe Potter—he did it," the injured lad had murmured, and these words were woven in the pattern of Ruth's dreams all night.

The little cottage was astir early and Ruth was no laggard. She came down to breakfast while the sun was just peeping above the house-tops and as she entered the sitting room she found an occupant at last in the little wheel-chair. It was the sharp, pale little face that confronted her above the warm wrapper and the rug that covered the lower part of the child's body; for child Mercy Curtis was, and little older than Ruth herself, although her face seemed so old.

To Ruth's surprise the first greeting of the invalid was a most ill-natured one. She made a very unpleasant face at the visitor, ran out her tongue, and then said, in her shrill, discordant voice:

"I don't like you at all—I tell you that, Miss!"

Alice B. Emerson

"I am sorry you do not like me," replied Ruth, gently. "I think I should like you if you'd let me."

"Yah!" ejaculated the very unpleasant, but much to be pitied invalid.

The mother and father ignored all this ill-nature on the part of the lame girl and were as kind and friendly with their visitor as they had been on the previous evening. Once during breakfast time (Mercy took hers from a tray that was fastened to her chair before her) the child burst out again, speaking to Ruth. There were eggs on the table and, pointing to the golden-brown fried egg that Mrs. Curtis had just placed upon Ruth's plate, Mercy snapped:

"Do you know what's the worst wish I'd wish on My Enemy?"

Ruth looked her astonishment and hesitated to reply. But Mercy did not expect a reply, for she continued quickly:

"I'd wish My Enemy to have to eat every morning for breakfast two soft fried eggs with his best clothes on—that's what I'd wish!"

And this is every word she would say to the visitor while Ruth remained. But Mr. Curtis bade Ruth good-bye very kindly when he hurried away to the station, and Mrs. Curtis urged her to come and see them whenever she came to town after getting settled at the Red Mill.

It was a fresh and lovely morning, although to the weather-wise the haze in the West foredoomed the end of the day to disaster. Ruth felt more cheerful as she crossed the railroad tracks and struck into the same street she had followed with the searching party the evening before. She could not mistake Doctor Davison's house when she passed it, and there was a fine big automobile standing before the gate where the two green lanterns were. But there was nobody in the car, nor did she see anybody about the doctor's house.

Beyond the doctor's abode the houses were far apart—farther and farther apart as she trudged on. Nobody noticed or spoke to the girl as she went on with her small bag—the bag that grew heavy, despite its smallness, as she progressed. And so she traveled two miles, or more, along the pleasant road. Then she heard the purring of an automobile behind her—the first vehicle that she had seen since leaving town.

It was the big gray car that had been standing before Doctor Davison's house when she had passed, and Ruth would have known the girl who sat at the steering wheel and was driving the car alone, even had Reno, the big mastiff, not sat in great dignity on the seat beside her. For no girl could look so much like Tom Cameron without being Tom Cameron's sister.

And the girl, the moment she saw Ruth on the road, retarded the speed of the machine. Reno, too, lost all semblance of dignity and would not wait for the car to completely stop before bounding into the road and coming to caress her hand.

"I know who you are!" cried the girl in the automobile. "You are Ruth Fielding."

She was a brilliant, black-eyed, vivacious girl, perhaps a year or more older than Ruth, and really handsome, having her brother's olive complexion with plenty of color in cheeks and lips. And that her nature was impulsive and frank there could be no doubt, for she immediately leaped out of the automobile, when it had stopped, and ran to embrace Ruth.

"Thank you! thank you!" she cried. "Doctor Davison has told

us all about you—and how brave you are! And see how fond Reno is of you! He knows who found his master; don't you, Reno?"

"Oh, dear me," said Ruth, breathlessly, "Doctor Davison has been too kind. I did nothing at all toward finding your brother—I suppose he is your brother, Miss?"

"How dare you 'Miss' me?" demanded the other girl, hugging her again. "You're a dear; I knew you must be! And I was running back and intended to stop at the Red Mill to see you. I took father to town this morning, as he had to take an early train to the city, and we wished to see Tom again,"

"He—he isn't badly hurt, then—your brother, I mean?" said Ruth, timidly.

"He is going to stay at the doctor's to-day, and then he can come home. But he will carry his arm in a sling for a while, although no bone was broken, after all. His head is badly cut, but his hair will hide that. Poor Tom! he is always falling down, or getting bumped, or something. And he's just as reckless as he can be. Father says he is not to be trusted with the car as much as I am."

"How—how did he come to fall over that bank?" asked Ruth, anxiously.

"Why—it was dark, I suppose. That was the way of it. I don't know as he really told me what made him do such a foolish thing. And wasn't it lucky Reno was along with him?" cried Tom's sister.

"Now, I see you remained in town over night. They thought somebody had come for yon and taken you out to the mill. Is Jabez Potter really your uncle?"

"Yes. He was my mother's uncle. And I have no other relative."

"Well, dear, I am more than sorry for you," declared the girl from the automobile. "And now we will climb right in and I'll take you along to the mill."

But whether she was sorry for Ruth Fielding's friendlessness, or sorry because she was related to Jabez Potter, the young traveler could not decide.

Alice B. Emerson

CHAPTER VI

THE RED MILL

"Now, my name's Helen, and you are Ruth," declared Miss Cameron, when she had carefully started the car once more. "We are going to be the very best of friends, and we might as well begin by telling each other all about ourselves. Tom and I are twins and he is an awful tease! But, then, boys are. He is a good brother generally. We live in the first yellow house on the right—up among the trees—beyond Mr. Potter's mill—near enough so that we can run back and forth and see each other just lots."

Ruth found herself warmly drawn toward this vivacious miss. Nor was she less frank in giving information about herself, her old home, in Darrowtown, that she still wore black for her father, and that she had been sent by her friends to Uncle Jabez because he was supposed to be better able to take care of and educate her. Helen listened very earnestly to the tale, but she shook her head at the end of it.

"I don't know," she said. "I don't want to hurt your feelings, Ruthie. But Jabez Potter isn't liked very well by people in general, although I guess he is a good miller. He is stingy—"

I must say it. He isn't given to kind actions, and I am

surprised that he should have agreed to take and educate you. Of course, he didn't have to."

"I don't suppose he did have to," Ruth said, slowly. "And it wasn't as though I couldn't have remained in Darrowtown. But Miss True Pettis—"

"Miss True?" repeated Helen, curiously.

"Short for Truthful. Her name is Rechelsea Truthful Tomlinson Pettis and she is the dearest little old spinster lady— much nicer than her name."

"Well!" ejaculated the amazed Helen.

"Miss True isn't rich. Indeed, she is very poor. So are Patsy Hope's folks—Patsy is really Patricia, but that's too long for her. And all the other folks that knew me about Darrowtown had a hard time to get along, and most of them had plenty of children without taking another that wasn't any kin to them," concluded Ruth, who was worldly wise in some things, and had seen the harder side of life since she had opened her eyes upon this world.

"But your uncle is said to be a regular miser," declared Helen, earnestly. "And he is so gruff and grim! Didn't your friends know him?"

"I guess they never saw him, or heard much about him," said Ruth, slowly. "I'm sure I never did myself."

"But don't you be afraid," said the other, warmly. "If he isn't good to you there are friends enough here to look out for you. I know Doctor Davison thinks you are very brave, and Daddy will do anything for you that Tom and I ask him to."

Alice B. Emerson

"I am quite sure I shall get on nicely with Uncle Jabez," she said. "And then, there is Aunt Alvirah."

"Oh, yes. There is an old lady who keeps house for Mr. Potter. And she seems kind enough, too. But she acts afraid of Mr. Potter. I don't blame her, he is so grim."

The automobile, wheeling so smoothly over the hard pike, just then was mounting a little hill. They came over the summit of this and there, lying before them, was the beautiful slope of farming country down to the very bank of the Lumano River. Fenced fields, tilled and untilled, checkered the slope, with here and there a white farmhouse with its group of outbuildings. There was no hamlet in sight, merely scattered farms. The river, swollen and yellow with the Spring rains, swept upon its bosom fence rails, hen-coops, and other flotsam of a Spring flood. Yonder, at a crossing, part of the bridge had been carried away.

"If the dam at Minturn goes, we shall be flooded all through this low land again," Helen Cameron explained. "I remember seeing this valley covered with water once during the Spring. But we live on the shoulder of Mount Burgoyne, and you see, even the mill sets on quite high ground."

Ruth's eyes had already seen and lingered upon the mill. It was a rambling structure, the great, splashing millwheel at the far end, the long warehouse in the middle, and the dwelling attached to the other end. There were barns, corn-cribs and other outbuildings as well, and some little tillable land connected with the mill; and all the buildings were vividly painted with red mineral paint, trimmed with white. So bright and sparkling was the paint that it seemed to have been put on over night.

"Mr. Potter is considered a good miller," said Helen, again;

"and he does not neglect his property. He is not miserly in that way. There isn't a picket off the fence, or a hinge loose anywhere. He isn't at all what you consider a miser must be and look like; yet he is always hoarding money and never spends any. But indeed I do not tell you this to trouble you, Ruthie. I want you to believe, my dear, that if you can't stand it at Mr. Potter's you can stand it at Mr. Cameron's—and you'll be welcome there.

"Our mother is dead. We talk of her a good deal, just as though she were living and had gone on a little journey somewhere, and we should see her again soon. God took her when Tom and I were only a few weeks old; but Daddy has made himself our playfellow and dear, dear friend; and there has always been Nurse Babette and Mrs. Murchiston—at least, Mrs. Murchiston has been with us since we can remember. But what Daddy says is law, and he said this morning that he'd like to have a girl like you come to our house to be company for me. It gets lonely for me sometimes, you see, for Tom doesn't want to play with girls much, now he is so big. Perhaps next fall I'll go away to boarding school—won't that be fun?"

"It will be fun for you, I hope, Helen," said Ruth, with rather a wistful smile. "I don't know where I shall go to school."

"There is your uncle now!" exclaimed Miss Cameron. "See that man in the old dusty suit?"

Ruth had already seen the tall, stoop-shouldered figure, who looked as though he had been powdered with flour, coming down the short path from one of the open doors of the mill to the road, where a little, one horse wagon stood. He bore a bag of meal or flour on his shoulder which he pitched into the wagon. The man on the seat was speaking as the automobile came to a stop immediately behind the wagon.

Alice B. Emerson

"Jefers pelters! Ef there's one thing yeou know how to do, it's to take toll, Jabe. Let the flour be poor, or good, there's little enough of it comes back to the man that raises the wheat."

"You don't have to bring your wheat here, Jasper Parloe," said the miller, in a strong, harsh voice. "There is no law compels ye."

"Yah!" snarled old Parloe. "We all know ye, Jabe Potter. We know what ye be." Potter turned away. He had not noticed the two girls in the automobile. But now Jasper Parloe saw them. "Ho!" he cried, "here's somebody else that will l'arn ter know ye, too. Didn't know you was ter hev comp'ny; did ye, Jabe? Here's yer niece, Jabe, come ter live on ye an' be an expense to ye," and so, chuckling and screwing up his mean, sly face, Parloe drove on, leaving the miller standing with arms akimbo, and staring at Ruth, who was slowly alighting from the automobile with her bag.

Helen squeezed her hand tightly as she got out "Don't forget that we are your friends, Ruthie," she whispered. "I'm coming by again this afternoon when I drive over to the station for father. If—if anything happens you be out here— now remember!"

What could possibly happen to her, Ruth could not imagine. She was not really afraid of Uncle Jabez. She walked directly to him, as he stood there, staring gloomily, in front of the Red Mill. He was not only tall and stoop-shouldered, and very dusty; but his dusty eyebrows almost met over his light blue eyes. He was lantern-jawed, and it did seem as though his dry, shaven lips had never in all his life wrinkled into a smile. His throat was wrinkled and scraggy and his head was plainly very bald on top, for the miller's cap he wore did not entirely cover the bald spot.

"I am Ruth Fielding, from Darrowtown," she said, in a voice that she controlled well. "I have come to—to live with you, Uncle Jabez."

"Where was you last night?" demanded the miller, without so much as returning her greeting. "Was you with them Camerons?"

"I stayed all night with the station master," she said, in explanation.

"What time did you get to the station?"

Ruth told him. Never once did his voice change or his grim look relax.

"I mistook the time of the train," he said, without expressing any sorrow.

"I—I hope you will be glad to have me come," the said. "Miss True—"

"You mean that old maid that wrote to me?" he asked, harshly.

"Miss True Pettis. She said she thought you would like to have me here as we were so near related."

"Not so near related as some," was all he said in reply to this. After a moment, he added: "You can go along to the house yonder. Aunt Alviry will show you what to do."

Ruth could not have said another word just then without breaking down and weeping, so she only nodded and turned to walk up a path toward the house door.

Alice B. Emerson

"One thing," urged the old man, before she had gone far. She turned to look at him and he continued: "One thing I want you to understand, if you live here you have got to work. I don't like no laggards around me."

She could only nod again, for her heart seemed to be right in her throat, and the sting of the tears she wanted to shed, but could not, almost blinded her as she went on slowly to the house door.

CHAPTER VII

AUNT ALVIRAH'S BACK AND BONES

Ruth came to the kitchen door and found that the lower half was closed; but she could see over the upper panel that had been flung wide to let in the sweet Spring air and sunlight. A little old woman was stooping to brush the rag carpet with a whisk broom and dustpan, and as she hobbled around the big stove and around the table, which was already set neatly for dinner, she was crooning to herself:

"Oh, my back and oh, my bones ! Oh, my back and oh, my bones!"

She was a very neat-looking old lady, with a kerchief crossed on her breast in the style of the old-fashioned Quakeresses. She was not much taller than Ruth herself, for when she stood upright—or as upright as she could stand—her eyes were just about on a level with Ruth's eyes looking in over the half door.

But the face of the old lady seemed, to the lonely, tear-filled girl, almost the gentlest, sweetest face she had ever seen, as it slowly smiled upon her. Aunt Alviry's welcome was like the daybreak.

Alice B. Emerson

"Bless us and save us!" ejaculated she, rising upright by degrees with her hand upon the back she had been apostrophizing. "If here isn't a pretty little creeter come to see her Aunt Alviry. How-de-do, girl?"

Ruth had set down her bag. Now she opened the door and stepped in. The smile of the old lady broke down every bit of fortitude the girl had left and she walked directly into Aunt Alviry's arms and burst into tears.

"There! there! Deary, deary me!" murmured the little old lady, patting her shoulder. "Somebody has been treating you badly, I know. And you've come right to your Aunt Alviry for comfort. And you've come to the right place, my pretty girl, for I've got tons of comfort for ye."

She found a chair and lowered herself into it, not without the formula which Ruth had heard before, of "Oh, my back and oh, my bones!" Ruth dropped on her knees before her, hid her face in the old lady's lap, and had her cry out. Meanwhile Aunt Alvirah seemed to have taken in several things about her guest that were significant. She touched the stuff of which Ruth's gown was made, and nodded; even the black hair-ribbon did not go unnoticed.

"Now," said Ruth, rising after a few moments, "I guess that's all of that foolishness. I—I don't usually cry, Aunt Alvirah."

"Pshaw, now! I could tell that," said the old lady, comfortably.

"I am going right to work to help you," said the girl. "I can stoop better than you can."

"I expect you can, you pretty creeter," admitted the old lady.

Ruth had already taken the brush and pan and was at work

upon the floor. The lady said: "You ain't familiar to me, child. You've lost some folks lately, I see. Do you live 'round here?"

The little girl stopped and looked up at her in surprise. "Why, don't you know about it?" she cried.

"Know about what, child?"

"Didn't you know I had come here to live with you?"

"Bless us and save us!" ejaculated Aunt Alvirah. "How did that happen?"

"Didn't my uncle tell you?" cried Ruth, much more surprised than the old lady.

"Who's your uncle, child?"

"Why, Mr. Potter—Uncle Jabez."

So astonished did the old lady appear to be that she started from her chair and her ejaculation was changed to a moan of pain as she murmured her old formula: "Oh, my back and oh, my bones!"

"Jabez ain't said a word to me about it. Why should he take anybody to help me? Is he struck with the fear o' his latter end?"

She said this in no cross-grained way, but because she was so amazed. She likewise stared harder and harder at her visitor.

"You ain't come from the poor farm, child?" she asked, finally.

Alice B. Emerson

The flush upon Ruth's cheek and the expression which came into her face told Aunt Alviry that she was wrong there.

"Not that you look like poorhouse breed—not at all. You're too pretty dressed and you're too well fed. I know what they be there, for I have been there myself. Yes, ma'am! Jabez Potter came after me to the poor farm. I was sickly, too. There's them that said he went to Doctor Davison first to find out if I was goin' to git well before he come arter me; but Jabez ain't never treated me noways but kind. Starn he is—by natur and by practice; an' clost he is in money matters. But he's been good to an old woman without a home who warn't neither kith nor kin to him."

Ruth listened to the first good word she had heard of Uncle Jabez, and the speech comforted her somewhat. Perhaps there was something better within the rough husk of Uncle Jabez, after all.

"I did not live near here," Ruth said, quietly. "But my papa and mama did. I came from Darrowtown."

Aunt Alviry opened wide her bright brown eyes, and still stared in wonder.

"My mother's name was Mary Potter, and she was Mr. Potter's niece. So he is my great-uncle."

"Bless us and save us!" ejaculated Aunt Alviry, again, shaking her head. "I never heard a word of it—never! I 'member Mary Potter, and a sweet, pretty child she was. But Jabez never had no fondness for any of his kin. You—you are all alone in the world, child?"

"All alone save for Uncle Jabez."

She had come near to the old woman again. As she dropped quietly on her knees Aunt Alviry gathered her head close to her bosom; but Ruth did not weep any more. She only said:

"I know I shall love you very, very much, dear Aunt Alvirah. And I hope I shall help your back and your bones a great deal, too!"

Alice B. Emerson

CHAPTER VIII

HOARDING UP: PASSIONS—MONEY—WATER

This was Ruth Fielding's introduction to the Red Mill, its occupants, and its surroundings. The spot was, indeed, beautiful, and an hour after she had arrived she knew that she would love it. The Lumano River was a wide stream and from the little window of the chamber that Aunt Alviry said would be her own, she could look both up and down the river for several miles.

Uncle Jabez had a young man to help him in the mill. It was true, Aunt Alviry said, that Jasper Parloe had worked for some time at the Red Mill; but he was quarrelsome and Mr. Potter had declared he was not honest. When the mill owner was obliged to be absent and people had come to have corn or wheat ground, paying for the milling instead of giving toll, Jasper had sometimes kept the money instead of turning it over to Mr. Potter. This had finally resulted in a quarrel between the two, and Mr. Potter had discharged Parloe without paying him for his last month's work.

The young newcomer had learned a great deal about the big mill and the homestead, and about the work Aunt Alviry had to do, before the first meal was prepared. She was of much assistance, too, and when Uncle Jabez came in, after washing at the pump, but bringing a cloud of flour with him on his clothes, the old woman was seated comfortably in her chair and Ruth "dished up the dinner."

At the end of his meal her uncle spoke just once to Ruth. "You have l'arned to work, I see. Your Aunt Alviry has trouble with her back and bones. If you make yourself of use to her you can stay here. I expect all cats to catch mice around the Red Mill. Them that don't goes into the sluice. There's enough to do here. You won't be idle for want of work."

And this was every word of his welcome, in a tone that showed neither interest nor care for the girl. It was what help she could be and how much he could save by her. It was plain enough that Uncle Jabez Potter was as saving as a person could possibly be. There was none too much food on the table, and Ruth watched the ravenous hunger of the hired man, when he came in, with a feeling as though she were watching a half-starved dog at his meal.

Jabez Potter was not like the misers Ruth had read about, save in his personal appearance. He was not well dressed, nor was he very clean. But naturally the mill-dust would stick to him and to his clothing. It seemed to have worked into the very texture of his skin during all the years he had controlled the mill, until he was all of a dead gray.

Sometimes there were half a dozen wagons or buggies waiting at the mill, and not all of them gave toll for their milling. Ruth, in the afternoon, and because it had begun to rain and she could not go out, went into the mill to quench her curiosity regarding it. She saw that there was a tiny office over the water, with a fireproof safe in it. Her uncle brought the money he took from his customers and put it in a little locked, japanned box, which he kept upon a shelf. The

Alice B. Emerson

safe appeared to be full of ledgers.

Farther down the mill was a wide door and platform over-hanging the water (this was below the dam) where flour and meal could be loaded upon barges for transportation to Osago Lake, some miles away. There were great bins of wheat and corn, many elevator pipes, several mills turning all the time, grinding different grains, and a great corn-sheller that went by power, and which the young man fed when he had nothing else to do.

All the time the building trembled and throbbed, and this throbbing was communicated to the house. As she sat with Aunt Alvirah, and sewed carpet-rags for a braided mat, the distant thunder of the mills and the trembling of the machinery made the whole house vibrate.

Late in the afternoon Ruth heard the honking of an auto horn and ran out upon the covered porch. Between the scuds of rain that drove along the valley she saw the gray automobile coming slowly past the mill. There was a man driving it now, and he stopped and let Helen Cameron out so that she could run up to great Ruth under the shelter of the porch.

"Oh, you dear! How are you getting on?" cried Helen, kissing her impulsively and as glad to see Ruth as though they had been separated for days instead of for only a few hours. "Colfax wanted to drive down to the station alone for Daddy—for we won't bring poor Tom home in this rain—but I just couldn't resist coming to see how you were getting on." She looked around with big eyes. "How does the Ogre treat you?" she whispered.

But Ruth could laugh now and did so, saying, cheerfully: "He hasn't eaten me up yet! And Aunt Alvirah is the dearest little lady who ever lived."

"She likes you, then?"

"Of course she does."

"I knew she would, she was bound to love you. But I don't know about the Ogre," and she shook her head. "But there! I must run. We don't want to be late for the train. That will put Daddy out. And I must stop and see Tom at the doctor's, too."

"I hope you will find your brother ever so mach better," cried Ruth, as her friend ran down the walk again.

"You'll see him come by here to-morrow, if it quits raining," returned Helen, over her shoulder.

But it did not stop raining that night, nor for a full week. The scuds of rain, blowing across the river, slapped sharply against the side of the house, and against Ruth's window all night. She did not sleep that first night as well as she had in the charitable home of the station master and his good wife. The evening meal had been as stiff and unpleasant as the noon meal. The evening was spent in the same room—the kitchen. Aunt Alviry knitted and sewed; Uncle Jabez pored over certain accounts and counted money very softly behind the uplifted cover of the japanned cash-box that he had brought in from the mill.

She got in time to know that cash-box very well indeed. It often came into the house under Uncle Jabez's arm at dinner, too. He scarcely seemed willing to trust it out of his sight. And Ruth was sure that he locked himself into his room with it at night.

A loaded shotgun lay upon rests over the kitchen door all the time, and there was a big, two-barreled, muzzle-loading pistol on the stand beside Uncle Jabez's bed. Ruth was much more afraid of these loaded weapons than she was of burglars. But the old man evidently expected to be attacked for his wealth at some time although, Aunt Alvirah told her, nobody had ever troubled him in all the years she had lived at the Red Mill.

So it was not fear of marauders that kept Ruth so wakeful on this first night under her uncle's roof. She thought of all the kind friends she had left in Darrowtown, and her long journey here, and her cold welcome to what she supposed would be her future home. Without Helen, and without Aunt Alvirah, she knew she would have gotten up, put on her clothing, packed her bag, and run away in the rain to some other place. She could not have stood Uncle Jabez alone.

Jabez Potter was hoarding up something besides money, too. Ruth did not understand this until it had already rained several days, and the roaring of the waters fretting against the river banks and against the dam, had become all but deafening in her ears.

Then, during a lull in the storm, and on the afternoon that Tom Cameron was taken home from Dr. Davison's, the old doctor himself stopped at the mill and shouted for Jabez to come out. The doctor drove a very fast red and white mare and had difficulty in holding her in, for she was eager to be moving.

Uncle Jabez came out and seemed to look upon the doctor in no very friendly way. Ruth, standing at the open door of the kitchen, could hear Dr. Davison's voice plainly.

"Jabez," he said, "do you know how the river is at Minturn?"

"No," returned the miller, briefly.

"It's higher than it's ever been. That dam is not safe. Why don't you let your water out so that, if Minturn should break, she'd have free sweep here and so do less damage below? Let this small flood out and when the greater one comes there'll be less danger of a disaster."

"And how do I know the Minturn dam will burst, Dr. Davison?" asked Mr. Potter, tartly.

"You don't know it. I'm only advising that precaution."

"And if it don't burst I'll have my pains for my trouble—and no water for the summer, perhaps. They wouldn't let me have water later, if I needed it."

"But you're risking your own property here."

"And it's mine to risk, Dr. Davison," said Potter, in his sullen way.

"But there are other people to think of—"

I don't agree with you," interrupted the miller. "I have enough to do to attend to my own concerns. I don't bother about other people's business."

"Meaning that I do when I speak to you about the water; eh?" said the old doctor, cheerfully. "Well, I've done my duty. You'll learn some time, Jabez."

He let out the impatient mare then, and the mud spattered from his wheels as he flew up the road toward Cheslow.

Alice B. Emerson

CHAPTER IX

THE CREST OF THE WAVE

The rain could not last forever; Nature must cease weeping some time. Just as girls, far away from their old homes and their old friends, must cease wetting their pillows with regretful tears after a time, and look forward to the new interests and new friends to which they have come.

Not that Ruth wept much. But the rainy days of that first week were necessarily trying. On Saturday, however, came a clear day. The sun shone, the drenched trees shook themselves, and the wind came and blew softly and warmly through their branches to dry the tender foliage. The birds popped out of their hiding-places and began to sing and chirp as though they never could be glad enough for this change in the weather.

There was so much to see from the kitchen door at the Red Mill that Ruth did not mind her work that morning. She had learned now to help Aunt Alvirah in many ways. Not often did the old lady have to go about moaning her old refrain:

"Oh, my back and oh, my bones! Oh, my back and oh, my bones!"

The housework was all done and the kitchen swept and as neat as a new pin when the gay tooting of the Cameron automobile horn called Ruth to the porch. There was only Helen on the front seat of the car; but in the tonneau was a bundled-up figure surmounted by what looked to be a scarlet cap which Ruth knew instantly must be Tom's. Ruth did not know many boys and, never having had a brother, was not a little bashful. Besides, she was afraid Tom Cameron would make much of her connection with his being found on the Wilkins Corners road that dark night, after his accident.

And there was another thing that made Ruth feel diffident about approaching the boy. She had borne it all the time in her mind, and the instant she saw Tom in the automobile it bobbed up to the surface of her thought again.

"It was Jabe Potter—he did it."

So, for more reasons than one, Ruth approached the motor car with hesitation.

"Oh, Ruth!" cried Helen, putting out a gauntleted hand to her. "So this horrid rain has not washed you away? You won't like the Red Mill if the weather keeps this way. And how do you get on?" she added, lowering her voice. "How about the Ogre?"

"He has not ground me into bread-flour yet," responded Ruth, smiling.

"I see he hasn't. You're just as plump as ever, so he hasn't starved you, either. Now, Ruth, I want you to know my brother Tom, whom you have met before without his having been aware of it at the time," and she laughed again.

Tom's left arm was in a sling, and the scarlet bandage around

Alice B. Emerson

his head made him look like a pirate; but he grinned broadly at Ruth and put out his lean brown hand.

"When I heard about you, Miss Fielding, I knew you were a spunky one," he said. "And anybody that Reno takes to, the way she did to you, is all right. Besides, Nell is just spoons on you already, and Nell, like Reno, doesn't take to every girl."

"The doctor said an outing in the car wouldn't hurt Tom," went on Helen, "and we're going to run up the valley road a way. Now Ruth Fielding, you get your hat and coat and come with us."

"I don't know that I may," Ruth said, timidly.

"I'll believe that he is an ogre then, and that you are kept a prisoner in this awful castle," cried Helen.

"I'd love to go," murmured Ruth.

"Then run and ask," urged her friend, while Tom added, good-naturedly:

"Yes, why not come along? Don't be afraid of Nell's driving. She handles the car all right."

Ruth knew that Uncle Jabez had gone to town. She had a feeling that he did not like the Camerons and might oppose her friendliness with them. But he was not at hand now to interfere with her innocent pleasures. She went in and asked Aunt Alvirah if she could take the ride.

"Why not, child? You've been the very best helpmate ever an old woman had—Oh, my back and oh, my bones! Run along and have your fun, deary. You need not be back till supper time. You have earned your little outing, that's sure and sartain."

Before Helen had picked her up on the road to the Red Mill that first day, Ruth had never ridden in a motor car. On that occasion they had traveled very slowly, while the girls talked. But now, when she was seated beside her new friend, Helen ran the auto on its high gear, and they shot away up the level river road at a pace that almost took Ruth's breath away,

"Up here among the foothills is the big Minturn Pond Dam," Tom said, leaning forward to speak to their guest. "It's twenty miles above your uncle's dam and is a deal bigger. And some say it is not safe—Wait, Nell! Slow down so that we can see the face of the dam from the Overlook."

The speed of the car was immediately reduced under Helen's manipulation, and then she swerved it into a short side road running toward the river, and they came out upon a little graveled plaza in the center of a tiny park, which gave a splendid view of the valley in both directions.

But the young people in the motor car turned their eyes to the west. There the face of the Minturn dam could be discerned; and even as they looked at it they seemed to see it changing—dissolving, covered with mist, and spouting geysers of what at first seemed like smoke. But it was Tom who realized the truth.

"She's burst!" he cried. "The old dam's burst! There she goes in a dozen places!"

Although they were several miles down the valley, the thunder of the bursting masonry now echoed in their ears. And up from the bottom of the wall, near its center, a great

Alice B. Emerson

geyser spouted. In a moment the wall crumbled and they saw tons upon tons of the masonry melt away. The waters of the pond burst through in a solid flood and charged down the valley, spreading wider and wider as it charged on, and bearing upon its crest every light and unstable structure found in its path.

It was a startling—a terrifying sight. No wonder the two girls cried out in alarm and clung together. The sight of the charging flood fascinated them.

But then they were aroused—and that within the first half minute of their terror—by Tom. He was trying, crippled as he was, to climb over into their seat.

"What are you doing, you foolish boy?" cried Helen. "Sit down."

"We've got to get out of here!" muttered the excited youth.

"Why, we are safe here. The water will never rise to this height."

"I know it! I know it!" groaned Tom, falling back in his seat and paling because of the pain from his arm, which he had twisted. "But don't you see? There are many down the valley who won't know of this until too late. Why, they can't see it at the bridge—at Culm Falls—until the flood is right upon them."

"It's true!" gasped Helen. "What shall we do?"

"We must warn them—we can warn them, can't we?" demanded Ruth. "This car runs so fast—you control it so well, Helen. Can't we warn them?"

"Try it, Sis!" shouted Tom. "You can do it!"

And already his sister, setting her teeth hard upon her lower lip, was backing and turning the motor car. In twenty seconds they were dashing off upon the track over which they had so recently come—on the road down the valley with the flood following fast behind them.

Alice B. Emerson

CHAPTER X

THE RACE

The two girls on the front seat of the flying automobile were not prepared for racing. Of course, Ruth Fielding had no proper automobile outfit, and Helen had not expected such an emergency when she had started with her crippled brother for this afternoon run. She had no goggles, nor any mask; but she had the presence of mind to raise the wind-shield.

Already they could have heard the steady roaring of the advancing flood had not the racing motor car drowned all other sounds. There was, however, no need to look behind; they knew the wave was there and that it was sweeping down the valley of the Lumano with frightful velocity.

Indeed, they were not at all sure for those first few miles whether they were traveling as fast as the flood, or not. Suppose the wave should reach and sweep away the bridge before they could cross the river? The thought was in the mind of both Helen and Ruth, whether Tom, on the rear seat, considered it or not. When they finally shot out of the woods and turned toward the toll-bridge, all glanced around. From here the upper reaches of the Lumano were plainly revealed. And extending clear across the valley was the foam-crested wave charging down upon the lowlands, but a number of miles away.

Here was the first house, too. They saw a man and woman and several children out front, staring at the automobile as it raced down the road. Perhaps they had been called from the house by the vibration of the bursting dam.

Tom sprang up in the car and pointed behind him, yelling:

"The flood! The flood!"

It is doubtful if they heard what he said; and they, too, were on a knoll and likely out of the reach of the water. But the three in the automobile saw the whole family turn and run for the higher ground behind their house. They understood the peril which menaced the whole valley.

In a flash the auto had turned the bend in the river road, and the occupants saw the toll-bridge and the peaceful hamlet of Culm Falls. There was no stir there. The toll-bridge keeper was not even out of his cottage, and the light and flimsy gates were down across the driveway at either end of the bridge. The bend in the river hid the advancing wall of water. Perhaps, too, it deadened the sound of the bursting dam and the roar of the waters.

There was another house at the bend. Helen tooted the automobile horn as though it had gone crazy. The raucous notes must of a certainty have awakened anybody but the Seven Sleepers. But the three in the car saw no sign of life about the premises. Helen had started to slow down; but Tom stopped her with a hand on her arm.

"Not here! Not here!" he yelled. "Get across the river first, Nell! That wave is coming!"

Indeed it was. And the toll-bridge keeper did not appear, and the gates were shut. But Helen Cameron was excited now and her racing blood was up. She never hesitated at the frail barrier, but drove straight through it, smashing the gate to kindling wood, and smashing their own wind shield as well.

Out ran the toll-man then; but they were half way across the bridge; he could barely have raised the other gate had he set about it instantly. So they went through that, too, leaving him bawling and shrieking after them, but soon to learn by looking up the river what Tom meant by his excited words as the motor car swept by.

Helen slowed down at the smithy. There were several men there and a number of wagons. The trio in the car screamed at them: "The dam has burst! The flood is coming!" and then started up again and swept through the little village, looking back to see the group at the smithy running in all directions to give the alarm

Now the road, clear to the Red Mill and beyond, ran within sight of the river. The mill was all of ten miles away. The valley was low here and as far as they could see ahead it broadened considerably on this side of the Lumano. But the hills arose abruptly on the farther bank and all the force and mass of the flood must sweep across these meadows.

As the car moved on, Helen tooted the horn constantly. Its blasts alone should have warned people of what threatened, without Tom's frantic shouts and gesticulations. They were obliged, however, to slow down before several houses to make the occupants understand their danger.

They were not half way to the Red Mill when the roar of the advancing tidal wave was apparent even above the noise of the auto. Then they saw the crest of the flood appear around the bend and the already heavily burdened waters dashed themselves upon the toll-bridge. It crumpled up and disappeared like a spider-web bridge, and the flood rolled on, the wave widening and overflowing the lowlands behind the automobile.

Ahead of them now upon the road there was a single foot-passenger—a man carrying a heavy basket. He seemed so far from the higher ground, and so determined to keep to the road, that Ruth cried out and laid her hand upon Helen's arm. The latter nodded and shut off the engine so that the automobile ran down and almost stopped by this pedestrian.

"Here, you!" shouted Tom, from the tonneau. "Get in here quick! There's no time to lose!"

Much of what he said was lost in the roaring of the waters; but the fellow understood him well enough, and scrambled into the car with his basket. It was Jasper Parloe, and the old man was shaking as with palsy.

"My goodness gracious!" he croaked, falling back in the seat as the car darted away again. "Ain't this awful? Ain't this jest awful?"

He was too scared, one would have supposed, to think of much else than the peril of the flood sweeping the valley behind them; yet he stared up at Tom Cameron again and again as the auto hurried them on toward the safety of the higher ground about the Red Mill, and there was something very sly in his look.

"Ye warn't hurt so bad then, arter all, was ye, Master Cameron?" he croaked.

"I reckon I shall live to get over it," returned the boy, shortly.

"But no thanks to Jabe Potter—heh? Ha! I know, I know!"

Tom stared in return angrily, but the old man kept shaking his head and smiling up at him slily and in such a significant way that, had the boy not been so disturbed by what was going on behind them, he certainly would have demanded to know what the old fellow meant.

But the car was getting close to the long hill that mounted to the crest on which the Red Mill stood. How much better would it have been for Jabez Potter and all concerned had he taken Doctor Davison's advice and let out the water behind his dam! But now he was not even at home to do anything before the thousands upon thousands of tons of water from the Minturn reservoir swept through the Red Mill dam.

They saw the foaming, yellow water spread over the country behind them; but within half a mile of the mill it gathered into narrower compass again because of the nature of the land, and the wave grew higher as it rushed down upon Potter's dam. The motor car puffed up the hill and halted before the mill door.

"Will we be safe here, Tom?" cried Helen, as pale as a ghost now, but too brave to give way. "Are we safe?"

"We're all right, I believe," said Tom.

Jasper Parloe was already out of the car and ran into the mill. Only the hired man was there, and he came to the door with a face whiter than it was naturally made by the flour dust.

"Come in, quick!" he cried to the young people. "This mill can't go—it's too solid."

Beyond the Red Mill the ground was low again; had the

Camerons tried to keep on the road for home the flood would have overtaken the car. And to take the road that branched off for Cheslow would have endangered the car, too. In a few seconds the knoll on which the mill stood was an island!

The girls and Tom ran indoors. They could hardly hear each other shout during the next few minutes. The waters rose and poured over the dam, and part of it was swept out. Great waves beat upon the river-wall of the mill. And then, with a tearing crash of rent timbers and masonry, the front of the little office and the storeroom, built out over the river, was torn away.

From that quarter Jasper Parloe ran, yelling wildly. Ruth saw him dart out of the far door of the mill, stooping low and with his coat over his head as though he expected the whole structure to fall about his ears.

But only that wall and the loading platform for the boats were sliced off by the flood. Then the bulk of the angry waters swept past, carrying all sorts of debris before it, and no farther harm was done to the mill, or to Mr. Potter's other buildings.

Alice B. Emerson

CHAPTER XI

UNCLE JABEZ IS EXCITED

So rapidly had all this taken place that the girls had remained in the mill. But now Ruth, crying: "Aunt Alvirah will be frightened to death, Helen!" led the way down the long passage and through the shed into the kitchen porch. The water on this side of the building had swept up the road and actually into the yard; but the automobile stood in a puddle only and was not injured.

Aunt Alviry was sitting in her rocker by the window. The old woman was very pale and wan. She had her Bible open on her knees and her lips trembled in a smile of welcome when the girls burst into the room.

"Oh, my dears! my dears!" she cried. "I am so thankful to see you both safe!" She started to rise, and the old phrase came to her lips: "Oh, my back and oh, my bones!"

Then she rose and hobbled across the room. Her bright little, birdlike eyes, that had never yet known spectacles, had seen something up the Cheslow road.

"Who's this a-coming? For the land's sake, what reckless-ness! Is that Jabez and his mules, Ruthie? Bless us and save us! what's he going to try and do?"

The two girls ran to the door. Down the hill thundered a farm wagon drawn by a pair of mules, said mules being on the dead run while their driver stood in the wagon and snapped his long, blacksnake whip over their ears. Such a descent of the hill was reckless enough in any case; but now, at the foot, rolled the deep water. It had washed away a little bridge that spanned what was usually a rill, but the banks of this stream being overflowed for yards on either side, the channel was at least ten feet deep.

It was Jabez Potter driving so recklessly down the hill from Cheslow.

"Oh, oh!" screamed the old lady. "Jabez will be killed! Oh, my back and oh, my bones! Oh, deary, deary me!"

She had crossed the porch and was hobbling down the steps. Her rheumatic twinges evidently caused her excruciating pain, but the fear she felt for the miller's safety spurred her to get as far as the fence. And there Ruth and Helen kept her from splashing into the muddy water that covered the road.

"You can do no good, Aunt Alvirah!" cried Ruth.

"The mules are not running away with him, Mrs. Boggs," urged Helen.

"They'll kill him! He's crazy! It's his money—the poor, poor man!"

It was evident that Aunt Alvirah read the miller's excitement aright. Ruth remembered the cash-box and wondered if it had been left in the mill while her uncle went to Cheslow? However that might be, her attention—indeed, the attention of everybody about the mill—was held by the reckless actions of Mr. Potter.

It was not fifteen minutes after the wave had hit the mill and torn away a part of the outer office wall and the loading platform, or wharf, when the racing mules came down to the turbulent stream that lay between the Cheslow road and the Red Mill. The frightened animals would have balked at the stream, but the miller, still standing in the wagon, coiled the whip around his head and then lashed out with it, laying it, like a tongue of living fire, across the mules' backs.

They were young animals and they had been unused, until this day, to the touch of the blacksnake. They leaped forward with almost force enough to break out of their harness, but landing in the deep water with the wagon behind them. So far out did they leap that they went completely under and the wagon dipped until the body was full of water.

But there stood the miller, upright and silent, plying the whip when they came to the surface, and urging them on. Ruth had noticed before this that Uncle Jabez was not cruel to his team, or to his other animals; but this was actual brutality.

However, the mules won through the flood. The turgid stream was not wide and it was not a long fight. But there was the peril of mules, wagon and man being swept out into the main stream of the flood and carried over the dam.

"He is awful! awful!" murmured Helen, in Ruth's ear, as they clung together and watched the miller and his outfit come through and the mules scramble out upon solid ground.

The miller had brought his half-mad team to the mill and pulled the mules down right beside the Cameron's automobile. Already the young fellow who worked for him had flown out of the mill to Jabez's assistance. He seized the frightened mules by their bits.

"How much has gone, boy?" cried Jabez, in a strained, hoarse voice.

"Not much, boss. Only a part of the office an'—"

The miller was already in at the door. In a moment, it seemed, he was back again, having seen the damage done by the flood to his building. But that damage was comparatively slight. It should not have caused the old man to display such profound despair.

He wrung his hands, tore off his hat and stamped upon it on the walk, and behaved in such a manner that it was little wonder Helen Cameron was vastly frightened. He seemed beside himself with rage and despair.

Ruth, herself torn by conflicting emotions, could not bear to see the old man so convulsed with what seemed to be anguish of spirit, without offering her sympathy. During this week that she had been at the Red Mill it could not be said that she had gained Uncle Jabez's confidence—that she had drawn close to him at all. But it was not for a will on her part to do so.

The girl now left Aunt Alvirah and Helen on the porch and walked straight down to the old man. She was beside him, with a hand upon his arm, before he was aware of her coming.

He stared at her so angrily—with such an expression of rage and hopelessness upon his face—that she was held speechless for a moment.

Alice B. Emerson

"What do you know about it, girl?" he demanded, hoarsely.

"About what, Uncle?" she returned.

"The box—the cash-box—my money!" he cried, in a low voice. "Do you know anything about it? Was it saved?"

"Oh, Uncle! We only got here in the automobile just in time to escape the flood. The office was wrecked at that very moment. Was the box there?"

"Gone! Gone!" he murmured, shaking his head; and turning on his heel, he strode into the mill.

The boy had taken the mules around to the stable. Ruth hesitated, then followed the old man into the mill. There Jabez confronted Tom Cameron, sitting on a sack of meal and watching the turbid waters falling over the dam.

"Ha! Young Cameron," muttered Uncle Jabez. "You didn't see the cash-box, of course?"

"Where was it?" asked Tom, quietly.

"In that office—on a shelf, with an old coat thrown over it. I believed it to be as safe there as in the house with nobody but an old woman to guard it."

"Better put your money in the bank, sir," said Tom, coolly.

"And have some sleek and oily scoundrel steal it, eh?" snarled Uncle Jabez.

"Well, the water stole it, I reckon," Tom said. "I'm sorry for you if there was much money in the box. But I know nothing about it. Jasper Parloe might have saved the box had be known about it; he was over there by the office when the water tore away the wall."

"Jasper Parloe!" ejaculated Uncle Jabez, starting. "Was he here?"

"He wasn't here long," chuckled Tom. "He thought the mill was going and he lit out in a hurry."

Uncle Jabez made another despairing gesture and walked away. Ruth followed him and her hands closed upon the toil-hardened fist clenched at his side.

"I'm sorry, Uncle," she whispered.

He suddenly stared down at her.

"There! I believe you be, child. But your being sorry can't help it none. The money's gone—hard it come and it's hard to part with in this way."

"Was it a large sum, Uncle?"

"All the ready cash I had in the world. Every cent I owned. That boy said, put it in a bank. I lost money when the Cheslow Bank failed forty year ago. I don't get caught twice in the same trap—no, sir! I've lost more this time; but no dishonest blackleg will have the benefit of it, that's sure. The river's got it, and nobody will ever be a cent the better off for it. All! All gone!"

He jerked his hand away from Ruth's sympathetic pressure and walked moodily away.

Alice B. Emerson

CHAPTER XII

THE CATASTROPHE

This was the beginning of some little confidence between Ruth and Uncle Jabez. He had not been quite so stern and unbending, even in his passion, as before. He said nothing more about the lost cash-box—Aunt Alviry dared not even broach the subject—but Ruth tried to show him in quiet ways that she was sorry for his loss.

Uncle Jabez was not a gentle man, however; his voice being so seldom heard did not make it the less rough and passionate. There were times when, because of his black looks, Ruth did not even dare address him. And there was one topic she longed to address him upon very much indeed. She wanted to go to school.

She had always been quick at her books, and had stood well in the graded school of Darrowtown. There was a schoolhouse up the road from the Red Mill—not half a mile away; this district school was a very good one and the teacher had called on Aunt Alvirah and Ruth liked her very much.

The flood had long since subsided and the repairs to the mill and the dam were under way. Uncle Jabez grew no more pleasant, however, for the freshet had damaged his dam so that all the water had to be let out and he might go into midsummer with such low pressure behind the dam that he could not run the mill through the drouth. This possibility, together with the loss of the cash-box, made him—even Aunt Alvirah admitted—"like a dog with a sore head." Nevertheless Ruth determined to speak to him about the school.

She chose an evening when the kitchen was particularly bright and homelike and her uncle had eaten his supper as though he very much enjoyed it. There was no cash-box for him to be absorbed in now; but every evening he made countless calculations in an old ledger which he took to bed with him with as much care as he had the money-box.

Before he opened his ledger on this evening, however, Ruth stood beside him and put a hand upon his arm.

"Uncle," she said, bravely, "can I go to school?"

He stared at her directly for a moment, from under his heavy brows; but her own gaze never wavered.

"How much schoolin' do you want?" he demanded, harshly.

"If you please Uncle Jabez, all I can get," replied Ruth.

"Ha! Readin', writin', an' mighty little 'rithmatic—we called 'em 'the three R's '—did for me when I was a boy. The school tax they put onto me ev'ry year is something wicked. And I never had chick nor child to go to their blamed old school."

"Let me go, Uncle, and so get some of your money back that way," Ruth said, quickly, and smiling in her little, birdlike way with her head on one side.

Alice B. Emerson

"Ha! I don't know about that," he growled, shaking his head. "I don't see what I'll be makin' out of it."

"Perhaps I can help you later, if you'll let me learn enough," she urged. "I can learn enough arithmetic to keep your books. I'll try real hard."

"I don't know about that," he said, again, eyeing her suspiciously. "The little money I make I kin keep watch of—when I'm here to watch it, that is. There ain't no book-keeping necessary in my business. And then—there's your Aunt Alviry. She needs you."

"Don't you go for to say that, Jabez," interposed the old woman, briskly. "That child's the greatest help that ever was; but she can do all that's necessary before and arter school, and on Saturdays. She's a good smart child, Jabez. Let her have a chance to l'arn."

"Ain't no good ever come of books," muttered the miller.

"Oh, Uncle! Just let me show you," begged the girl, in her earnestness clinging to his arm with both hands.

He looked down for a moment at her hands as though he would fling off her hold. But he thought better of it, and waited fully a minute before he spoke.

"You know your Aunt Alviry needs ye," he said. "If you kin fix it with her, why I don't see as I need object."

"Will it be too much trouble for you to get my trunk, Uncle, so that I can begin going to school next week?" Ruth asked.

"Ain't you got nothin' to wear to school?" he said. "It's dress; is it? Beginning that trouble airly; ain't ye?"

He seemed to be quite cross again, and the girl looked at him in surprise.

"Dear Uncle! You will get the trunk from the station, won't you?"

"No I won't," he said. "Because why? Because I can't."

"You can't?" she gasped, and even Aunt Alvirah looked startled.

"That's what I said."

"Why—why can't you?" cried Ruth. "Has something happened to my trunk?"

"That's jest it—and it warn't no fault o' mine," said the miller. "I got the trunk like I said I would and it was in the wagon when we came down the hill yonder

"Oh, oh!" gasped Ruth, her hands clasped. "You don't mean when you ran the mules into the water, Uncle?"

"I had to get to my mill. I didn't know what was being done over here," he said, uglily. "And didn't I lose enough? What's the loss of some old rags, and a trunk, 'side of my money?"

He said it with such force, and with so angry a gesture, that she shrank back from him. But her pain and disappointment were so strong that she had to speak.

"And the trunk was washed out of the wagon, Uncle Jabez? It's gone?"

"That's what happened to it, I suppose," he grunted, and dropping his head, opened the ledger and began to study the

　　　　　Alice B. Emerson

long lines of figures there displayed. Not a word to show that he was sorry for her loss. No appreciation of the girl's pain and sorrow. He selfishly hugged to him the misfortune of his own loss and gave no heed to Ruth.

But Aunt Alvirah caught her hand as she passed swiftly. The old woman carried the plump little hand to her lips in mute sympathy, and then Ruth broke away even from her and ran upstairs to her room. There she cast herself upon the bed and, with her sobs smothered in the pillows, gave way to the grief that had long been swelling her heart to the bursting point.

CHAPTER XIII

BUTTER AND BUTTERCUPS

Such little keepsakes as remained of her father and mother—their photographs, a thin old bracelet, her mother's wedding ring, her father's battered silver watch had fortunately been in Ruth's bag. Those keepsakes had been too precious to risk in the trunk and in the baggage car. And how glad the girl was now that she had thus treasured these things.

But the loss of the trunk, with all her clothing—common though that clothing had been—was a disaster that Ruth could not easily get over. She cried herself to sleep that night and in the morning came down with a woebegone face indeed. Uncle Jabez did not notice her, and even Aunt Alvirah did not comment upon her swollen eyes and tear-streaked countenance. But the old woman, if anything, was kinder than ever to her.

It was Saturday, and butter day. Uncle Jabez owned one cow, and since Ruth had come to the mill it was her work twice a week to churn the butter. The churn was a stone crock with a wooden dasher and Ruth had just emptied in the thick cream when Helen Cameron ran in.

"Oh, Ruth!" she cried. "You're always busy—especially if I

chance to want you at all particularly."

"If you will be a drone yourself, Helen, you must expect to be always hunting company," laughed Ruth. "Just what is troubling Miss Cameron at present?"

"We're going to dress the Cove Chapel for to-morrow. You know, I told you our guild attends to the decoration of the chapel and I've just set my heart on making a great pillow of buttercups. The fields are full of them. And Tom says he'll help. Now, you'll come; won't you?"

"If I come for buttercups it will have to he after the butter comes!" returned Ruth, laughing.

She had begun to beat the dasher up and down and little particles of cream sprayed up through the hole in the cover of the jar, around the handle of the dasher. Helen looked on with growing interest.

"And is that the way to make butter?" she asked. "And the cream's almost white. Our butter is yellow—golden. Just as golden as the buttercups. Do you color it?"

"Not at this time of year. I used to help Miss True make butter. She had a cow. She said I was a good butter maker. You see, it's all in the washing after the butter comes. You wait and see."

"But I want to pick buttercups—and Tom is waiting down by the bridge."

"Can't help it. Butter before buttercups," declared Ruth, keeping the dasher steadily at work. "And then, Aunt Alvirah may want me for something else before dinner."

"We've got dinner with us—or, Tom has. At least, Babette put us up a basket of lunch."

"Oh! A picnic!" cried Ruth, flushing with pleasure. This visit had driven out of her mind —for the time, at least—her trouble of overnight.

"I'm going to ask Aunt Alviry for you," went on Helen, and skipped away to find the little old woman who, despite the drawback of "her back and her bones" was a very neat and particular housekeeper. She was back in a few moments.

"She says you can go, just as soon as you get the butter made. Now, hurry up, and let us get into the buttercup field, which is a whole lot nicer than the butter churn and—Oh! it smells much nicer, too. Why, Ruth, that cream actually smells sour!"

"I expect it is sour," laughed her friend. "Didn't you know that sweet butter comes from sour cream? And that most nice things are the result of hard work? The sweet from the bitter, you know."

"My! how philosophical we are this morning. Isn't that butter ever coming?"

"Impatience! Didn't you ever have to wait for anything you wanted in your life?"

"Why, I've got to wait till next fall before I go to Briarwood Hall. That's a rhyme, Ruthie; it's been singing itself over and over in my mind for days. I'm really going to boarding school in the autumn. It's decided. Tom is going to the military academy on the other side of Osago Lake. He'll be within ten miles of Briarwood."

Alice B. Emerson

Ruth's face had lost its brightness as Helen said this. The word "school" had brought again to the girl's mind her own unfortunate position and Uncle Jabez's unkindness.

"I hope you will have a delightful time at Briarwood," Ruth said, softly. "I expect I shall miss you dreadfully."

"Oh, suppose the Ogre should send you to school there, too!" cried Helen, with clasped hands. "Wouldn't that be splendid!"

"That would be beyond all imagination," said Ruth, shaking her head. "I—I don't know that I shall be able to attend the balance of the term here."

"Why not?" demanded Helen. "Won't he let you?"

"He has said I could." Ruth could say no more just then. She hid her face from her friend, but made believe that it was the butter that occupied her attention. The dasher began to slap, slap, slap suggestively in the churn and little particles of beaten cream began to gather on the handle of the dasher.

"Oh!" cried Helen. "It's getting hard!"

"The butter is coming. Now a little cold water to help it separate. And then you shall have a most delicious glass of buttermilk."

"No, thank you!" cried Helen. "They say it's good for one to drink it. But I never do like anything that's good for me."

"Give it to me, Ruth," interposed another voice, and Tom put a smiling face around the corner of the well. "I thought you were never coming, Miss Flyaway," he said, to his sister.

"Butter before buttercups, young man," responded Helen, primly. "We must wait for Ruth to—er—wash the butter, is it?"

"Yes," said her friend, seriously, opening the churn and beginning to ladle out the now yellow butter into a wooden bowl.

"May I assist at the butter's toilet?" queried Tom, grinning.

"You may sit down and watch," said his sister, in a tone intended to quell any undue levity on her brother's part.

Ruth had rolled her sleeves above her elbows, so displaying her pretty plump arms, and now worked and worked the butter in cold water right "from the north side of the well" as though she were kneading bread. First she had poured Tom a pitcher of the fresh buttermilk, and given him a glass. Even Helen tasted a little of the tart drink.

"Oh, it's ever so nice, I suppose," she said, with a little grimace; "but I much prefer my milk sweet."

Again and again Ruth poured off the milky water and ran fresh, cold water upon her butter until no amount of kneading and washing would subtract another particle of milk from the yellow ball. The water was perfectly clear.

"Now I'll salt it," she said; "and put it away until this afternoon, and then I'll work it again and put it down in the butter-jar. When I grow up and get rich I am going to have a great, big dairy; with a herd of registered cattle, and I'm going to make all the butter myself."

"And Tom's going to raise horses. He's going to own a stock farm—so he says. You'd better combine interests," said

Alice B. Emerson

Helen, with some scorn. "I like horses to ride, and butter to eat, but—well, I prefer buttercups just now. Hurry up, Miss Slow-poke! We'll never get enough flowers for a pillow."

So Ruth cleaned her face, taking a peep into the glass in the kitchen to make sure, before going out to her friends. Tom looked at her with plain approval, and Helen jumped up to squeeze her again.

"No wonder Aunt Alvirah calls you 'pretty creetur'," she whispered in Ruth's ear. "For that's what you are." Then to Tom: "Now young man, have you the lunch basket?"

"What there is left of it is in charge of Reno down at the bridge," he replied, coolly.

They found the huge mastiff lying with the napkin-covered basket between his forepaws, on the grass by the water side. Reno was growling warningly and had his eyes fixed upon a figure leaning upon the bridge railing.

"That there dawg don't seem ter take to me," drawled Jasper Parloe, who was the person on the bridge. "He needn't be afraid. I wouldn't touch the basket."

"You won't be likely to touch it while Reno has charge of it," said Tom, quietly, while the girls passed on swiftly. Neither Ruth nor Helen liked to have anything to do with Parloe. When Tom released Reno from his watch and ward, the dog trotted after Ruth and put his nose into her hand.

"Ye been up ter the mill, hev ye?" queried Parloe, eyeing Tom Cameron aslant. "ye oughter be gre't friends with Jabe Potter. Or has he squared hisself with ye?"

"Say, Mister Parloe," said Tom, sharply, "you've been

hinting something about the miller every time you've seen me lately

"Only since yeou was knocked down that bank inter the gully, an' yer arm an' head hurt. There warn't nothin' about Jabe ter interest yeou afore that," returned Parloe, quickly.

Tom flushed suddenly and he looked at the old fellow with new interest.

"Just what do you mean?" he asked, slowly.

"Ye know well enough. Your dad, Tom Cameron, is mighty riled up over your bein' hurt. I heered him say that he'd give a ten-dollar note ter know who it was drove by ye that night and crowded ye inter the ditch. Would you give more than that not ter have it known who done it?"

"What do you mean?" exclaimed Tom, angrily.

"I guess ye like this here gal that's cone to live on Jabez, purty well; don't ye—yeou an' yer sister?" croaked old Parloe. "Wal, if your dad an' the miller gits inter a row—comes ter a clinch, as ye might say—yeou an' yer sister won't be let ter hev much ter do with Ruth, eh, now?"

"I don't know that that's so," Tom said doggedly.

"Oh, yes, ye do. Think it over. Old Jabe will put his foot right down an' he'll stop Ruth havin' anything ter do with ye—ye know it! Wal, now; think it over. I got a conscience, I have," pursued Parloe, cringing and rubbing his hands together, his sly little eyes sparkling. "I r'ally feel as though I'd oughter tell yer dad who it was almost run ye down that night and made ye fall into the gully."

Alice B. Emerson

"You mean, you'd like to handle Dad's ten dollars!" cried Tom, angrily.

Parloe smirked and still rubbed his hands together. "Don't matter a mite whose ten dollars I handle," he said, suggestively. "Your ten dollars would be jest as welcome to me as your Dad's, Master Cameron."

"Ten dollars is a lot of money," said Tom.

"Yes. It's right smart. I could make use of it I'm a poor man, an' I could use it nicely," admitted the sly and furtive Parloe.

"I haven't got so much money now," growled the boy.

"Yeou kin get it, I warrant."

"I suppose I can." He drew his purse from his pocket. "I've got three dollars and a half here. I'll have the rest for you on Monday."

"Quite correct," said Jasper Parloe, clutching eagerly at the money. "I'll trust ye till then—oh, yes! I'll trust ye till then."

CHAPTER XIV

JUST A MATTER OF A DRESS

"Well, I really believe, Tommy Cameron!" cried his sister Helen, when he overtook the girls and Reno, swinging the basket recklessly, "that you are developing a love for low company. I don't see how you can bear to talk with that Jasper Parloe."

"I don't see how I can, either," muttered Tom, and he was rather silent—for him—until they were well off the road and the incident at the bridge was some minutes behind them.

But the day was such a glorious one, and the fields and woods were so beautiful, that no healthy boy could long be gloomy. Besides, Tom Cameron had assured his sister that he thought Ruth Fielding "just immense," and he was determined to give the girl of the Red Mill as pleasant a time as possible.

He worked like a Trojan to gather buttercups, and after they had eaten the luncheon old Babette had put up for them (and it was the very nicest and daintiest luncheon that Ruth Fielding had ever tasted) he told the girls to remain seated on the flat stone he had found for them and weave the foundation for the pillow while he picked bushels upon

Alice B. Emerson

bushels of buttercups.

"You'll need a two-horse load, anyway to have enough for a pillow of the size Nell has planned," he said, grinning. "And perhaps she'll finish it if you help her, Ruth. She's always trying to do some big thing and 'falling down' on it."

"That's not so, Master Sauce-box!" cried his sister.

Tom went off laughing, and the two girls set to work on the great mass of buttercups they had already picked. They grew so large, and were so dewey and golden, that a more brilliant bed of color one could scarce imagine than the pillow, as it began to grow under the dexterous hands of Helen and Ruth. And, being alone together now, they began to grow confidential.

"And how does the Ogre treat you?" asked Helen. "I thought, when I came this morning, that you had been feeling badly."

"I am not very happy," admitted Ruth.

"It's that horrid Ogre!" cried Helen.

"It isn't right to call Uncle Jabez names," said Ruth, quietly. "He is greatly to be pitied, I do believe. And just now, particularly so."

"You mean because of the loss of that cash-box?"

"Yes."

"Do you suppose there was much in it?"

"He told me that it contained every cent he had saved in all these years."

"My!" cried Helen. "Then he must have lost a fortune! He has been a miser for forty years, so they say."

"I do not know about that," Ruth pursued. "He is harsh and—and he seems to be very selfish. He—he says I can go to school, though."

"Well, I should hope so!" cried Helen.

"But I don't know that I can go," Ruth continued, shaking her head.

"For pity's sake I why not?" asked her friend.

Then, out came the story of the lost trunk. Nor could Ruth keep back the tears as she told her friend about Uncle Jabez's cruelty.

"Oh, oh, oh!" cried Helen, almost weeping herself. "The mean, mean thing! No, I won't call him Ogre again; he isn't as good as an Ogre. I—I don't know what to call him!"

"Calling him names won't bring back my trunk, Helen," sobbed Ruth.

"That's so. I—I'd make him pay for it! I'd make him get me dresses for those that were lost."

"Uncle is giving me a home; I suppose he will give me to wear all that he thinks I need. But I shall have to wear this dress to school, and it will soon not be fit to wear anywhere else."

"It's just too mean for anything, Ruth! I just wish—"

What Miss Cameron wished she did not proceed to explain.

Alice B. Emerson

She stopped and bit her lip, looking at her friend all the time and nodding. Ruth was busily wiping her eyes and did not notice the very wise expression on Helen's face.

"Look out! here comes Tom," whispered Helen, suddenly, and Ruth made a last dab at her eyes and put away her handkerchief in a hurry.

"Say! ain't you ever going to get that thing done?" demanded Tom. "Seems to me you haven't done anything at all since I was here last."

The girls became very busy then and worked swiftly until the pillow was completed. By that time it was late afternoon and they started homeward. Ruth separated from Helen and Tom at the main road and walked alone toward the Red Mill. She came to the bridge, which was at the corner of her uncle's farm, and climbed the stile, intending to follow the path up through the orchard to the rear of the house—the same path by which she and her friends had started on their little jaunt in the morning.

The brook which ran into the river, and bounded this lower end of Mr. Potter's place, was screened by clumps of willows. Just beyond the first group of saplings Ruth heard a rough voice say:

"And I tell you to git out! Go on the other side of the crick, Jasper Parloe, if ye wanter fish. That ain't my land, but this is."

"Ain't ye mighty brash, Jabe?" demanded the snarling voice of Parloe, and Ruth knew the first speaker to be her uncle. "Who are yeou ter drive me away?"

"The last time ye was at the mill I lost something—I lost

more than I kin afford to lose again," continued Uncle Jabez. "I don't say ye took it. They tell me the flood took it. But I'm going to know the right of it some time, and if you know more about it than you ought—"

"What air ye talkin' about, Jabe Potter?" shrilled Parloe. "I've lost money by you; ye ain't never paid me for the last month I worked for ye."

"Ye paid yerself—ye paid yerself," said Jabe, tartly. "And if ye stole once ye would again—"

"Now stop right there, Jabe Potter!" cried Parloe, and Ruth knew that he had stepped closer to Mr. Potter, and was speaking in a trembling rage. "Don't ye intermate an' insinerate; for if ye do, I kin fling out some insinerations likewise. Yeou jest open yer mouth about me stealin' an' I'll put a flea in old man Cameron's ear. Ha! Ye know what I mean. Better hev a care, Jabe Potter—better hev a care!"

There was silence. Her uncle made no reply, and Ruth, fearing she would be seen, and not wishing to be thought an eavesdropper (although the conversation had so surprised and terrified her that she had not thought what she did, before) the girl ran lightly up the hill, leaving the two old men to their wrangle. When Uncle Jabez came in to supper that evening his scowl was heavier than usual, if that were possible, and he did not speak to either Ruth or Aunt Alvirah all the evening.

Alice B. Emerson

CHAPTER XV

IN SCHOOL

Ruth thought it all over, and she came to this conclusion: Uncle Jabez had given his permission—albeit a grumpy one—and she would begin school on Monday. The black cloth dress that was so shabby and would look so odd and proverty-stricken among the frocks of the other girls (for she had watched them going to and from school, and already knew some of them to speak to) would have to be worn, if possible, through the term. Perhaps Uncle Jabez might notice how shabby she looked, finally, and give her something more appropriate to wear. Especially as it had been through him that her other frocks were lost.

But it was not an easy thing to face a whole schoolroom full of girls and boys—and most of them strangers to her—looking so "dowdyish." Ruth's love of pretty things was born in her. She had always taken pride in her appearance, and she felt her shortcomings in this line quicker and more acutely than most girls of her age.

She faced the school on Monday morning and found it not so hard as she had supposed. Miss Cramp welcomed her kindly, and put her through quite a thorough examination to decide her grade. The Darrowtown schools had been so good that

Ruth was able to take a high place in this one, and the teacher seated her among the most advanced of her pupils, although Ruth was younger than some of them.

The fact that Ruth was well grounded in the same studies that the scholars at this district school were engaged in, made a difficulty for her at the start. But she did not know it then. She only knew that Miss Cramp, seating her pupils according to their grade, sent her to an empty seat beside one of the largest girls—Julia Semple.

A good many of the girls stared at the new-comer with more than ordinary attention; but Julia immediately turned her back on her new seatmate. Ruth did not, however, give Julia much attention at the time. She was quite as bashful as most girls of her age; and, too, there were many things during that first session to hold her attention. But at recess she found that Julia walked away from her without a word and that most of the girls who seemed to be in her grade kept aloof, too. As a stranger in the school the girl from the Red Mill felt no little unhappiness at this evident slight; but she was too proud to show her disappointment. She made friends with the younger girls and was warmly welcomed in their games and pastimes.

"Julia's mad at you, you see," one of her new acquaintances confided to Ruth.

"Mad at me? What for?" asked the surprised new scholar.

"Why, that seat was Rosy Ball's. Rosy has gone away to see her sister married and she's coming back to-morrow. If you hadn't come in to take her place, Rosy would have been let sit beside Julia again, of course, although like enough she's fallen behind the class. Miss Cramp is very strict."

"But I didn't know that. I couldn't help it," cried Ruth.

"Just the same, Julia says she doesn't like you and that you're a nobody—that Jabe Potter has taken you in out of charity. And Julia pretty nearly bosses everything and everybody around this school. Her father, Mr. Semple, you see, is chairman of the school board."

Her plain-spoken friend never realized how much she was hurting Ruth by telling her this. Ruth's pride kept her up, nor would she make further overtures toward friendship with her classmates. She determined, during those first few days at the district school, that she would do her very best to get ahead and to win the commendation of her teacher. There was a splendid high school at Cheslow, and she learned that Miss Cramp could graduate pupils from her school directly into the Cheslow High. It was possible, the teacher assured her, for Ruth to fit herself for such advancement between that time and the fall term.

It seemed as though Ruth could never make her crotchety old uncle love her. As time passed, the loss of his cash-box seemed to prey upon the miller's mind more and more. He never spoke of it in the house again; it is doubtful if he spoke of it elsewhere. But the loss of the money increased (were that possible) his moroseness. He often spoke to neither the girl nor Aunt Alvirah from sunrise to sunset.

But although Uncle Jabez was so moody and so unkind to her, in the little old woman, whose back and whose bones gave her so much trouble, Ruth found a loving and thoughtful friend. Aunt Alvirah was as troubled at first about Ruth's lack of frocks as the girl was herself. But before Ruth had been attending school a week, she suddenly became very light-hearted upon the question of dress.

"Now, don't you fret about it, deary," said Aunt Alviry, wagging her head knowingly. "Gals like you has jest got ter hev frocks, an' the good Lord knows it, jest the same as He knows when a sparrer falls. There'll be a way pervided— there'll be a way pervided. Ef I can't make ye a purty dress, 'cause o' my back an' my bones, there's them that kin. We'll hev Miss 'Cretia Lock in by the day, and we'll make 'em."

"But, dear," said Ruth, wonderingly, "how will we get the goods—and the trimmings—and pay Miss Lock for her work?"

"Don't you fret about that. Jest you wait and see," declared Aunt Alvirah, mysteriously.

Ruth knew very well that the old woman had not a penny of her own. Uncle Jabez would never have given her a cent without knowing just what it was for, and haggling over the expenditure then, a good deal. To his view, Aunt Alviry was an object of his charity, too, although for more than ten years the old woman had kept his house like wax and had saved him the wages of a housekeeper.

This very day, on coming home from school, Ruth had met Doctor Davison coming away from the Red Mill. She thought the red and white mare, that was so spirited and handsome, had been tied to the post in front of the kitchen door, and that the physician must have called upon Aunt Alvirah.

"So this is the young lady who wouldn't stop at my house but went to Sam Curtis' to stay all night," he said, holding in the mare and looking down at Ruth. "And you haven't been past the gate with the green eyes since?"

"No, sir," Ruth said, timidly. "I have never even been

to town."

"No. Or you would not have failed to see the Curtises again. At least, I hope you'll see them. Mercy has never ceased talking about you."

"The lame girl, sir?" cried Ruth, in wonder. "Why, she spoke awfully unkindly to me, and I thought her mother only thought I would feel bad and wanted to smooth it over, when she asked me to come again."

"No," said the doctor, seriously, shaking his head. "Nobody knows Mercy like her mother. That's not to be expected. She's a poor, unfortunate, cramp-minded child. I've done what I can for her back—she has spinal trouble; but I can do little for Mercy's twisted and warped mind. She tells me she has cramps in her back and legs and I tell her she has worse cramps in her mind. Bright! Why, child, she knows more than most grown folks. Reads every book she can get hold of; there is scarcely a child in the Cheslow High School who could compete with her for a month in any study she had a mind to take hold of. But," and the doctor shook his head again, "her mind's warped and cramped because of her affliction."

"I pitied her," said Ruth, quietly.

"But don't tell her so. Go and see her again—that's all. And mind you don't come to town without turning in at the gate with the green eyes;" and so saying he let the eager mare out and she swiftly carried him away.

It was after this Aunt Alvirah seemed so confident that a way would be provided for Ruth to get the frocks that she so sadly needed. On the very next day, when Ruth came home from school, she found the little old lady in a flutter of excitement.

"Now, Ruthie," she whispered, "you mustn't ask too many questions, and I'll surely tell ye a gre't secret, child."

"It must be something very nice, Aunt Alviry, or you'd never be like this. What is it?"

"Now Ruthie, you mustn't ask too many questions, I tell you. But to make no secret of it, for secrets I do despise, somebody's made you a present."

"Made me a present?" gasped Ruth.

"Now, careful about questions," warned Aunt Alvirah. "I told you that a way would be pervided for you to have frocks. And it is true. You are a-goin' to have 'em."

"Auntie! New frocks!"

"Just as good as new. Ev'ry bit as good as new. Somebody that's—that's seen ye, deary, and knows how badly you want to go to school, and that you need dresses, has given you three."

"My goodness me!" cried Ruth, clasping her hands. Not three?"

"Yes, my dear. And they're jest as good as new—about. 'Cretia Lock won't be two days fixin' 'em over to fit you. And you won't mind, deary, if the little girl who wore them before you is—is—Well, deary, she won't never want them any more."

"Oh, my dear!" cried Ruth. "Three frocks all at once! And—and I'm not to ask who gave them to me?"

"That's it. You're not to ask that. I'll git 'em and show you—
Oh, my back and oh, my bones! Oh, my back and oh, my
bones!" the old lady added, starting from her chair and
hobbling out of the room.

Ruth was so amazed that she hardly knew what her other
feelings at the moment might be. But there had sprung into
her mind, full-fledged, the suspicion that Doctor Davison
had been the donor of the frocks. Perhaps he had had a little
girl sometime, who had died. For Ruth had quite decided,
from what Aunt Alvirah said, that the girl who had formerly
worn the frocks in question was no longer upon earth.

CHAPTER XVI

BEHIND THE GREEN LAMPS

Aunt Alvirah returned in a short time with such a pile of pretty colors over her arm that Ruth gasped with delight, she couldn't help it The dresses were all nice ginghams, each of a different color, nicely trimmed and delightfully made. They were not too fancy for school wear, and they were good, practical frocks.

Ruth had worn her little black and white frocks at school while she was still in Darrowtown, and had she remained longer Miss True Pettis would have helped her to make other frocks in colors. It is a sad thing to see a child in black, or black and white, and Ruth's father had been dead now six months.

"Ye needn't be scart at the colors, child," said old Aunt Alviry. "Here's this pretty lavender. We'll make that over first. 'Cretia Lock will be here to-morrow and we'll make a big beginnin'."

"But what will uncle say?" gasped Ruth, almost bursting with questions, but being debarred from asking the most important ones.

Alice B. Emerson

"Don't you fret about your Uncle Jabez. He ain't got nothin' ter do with it," declared the little old woman, firmly. "Nor he won't say nothin'."

Which was very true. Uncle Jabez seldom spoke to his niece now. His moodiness grew upon him as time passed. And in the evening, as he sat over his endless calculations at the kitchen table, the girl and the old woman scarcely dared speak to each other save in whispers.

Miss Lock worked three days, instead of two, at the Red Mill, helping Aunt Alvirah "dress-make." How she was paid, Ruth did not know; but she feared that the pennies Aunt Alvirah saved from her egg and chicken money had done this. However, the shabby black frock was put away and Ruth blossomed out into as pretty an appearance as any girl attending Miss Cramp's school.

But she did not make friends among her classmates. Julia Semple had such influence that she seemed to have set all the girls of the higher class in the district school against Ruth. Julia herself could not pass Ruth without tossing her head and staring at her haughtily; and sometimes she would whisper to her companions and look at the girl from the Red Mill in so scornful a way that Ruth could not help feeling uncomfortable.

Indeed, Ruth would have lacked almost all young company had it not been for Helen Cameron and Tom. Tom didn't think much of "playing with girls;" but he could always be depended upon to do anything Ruth and Helen wanted him to. Helen was at the Red Mill often after Ruth's school hours, and seldom did a Saturday pass that the two chums did not spend at least half the day together. Aunt Alvirah declared Ruth should have Saturday afternoons to herself, and often Helen came in her little pony carriage and drove Ruth about the country. There was a fat old pony named Tubby that drew the phaeton, and Tubby jogged along the pleasant country roads with them in a most delightfully gypsyish way.

One Saturday afternoon they went to town. Ruth had never seen Cheslow save on the night of her arrival and on the following morning, when she had started directly after breakfast at the station master's house to walk to the Red Mill.

"Why, you'll like Cheslow," declared Helen, in her enthusiastic way. "It's just as pretty as it can be—you'll love it! I often drive in to shop, and sometimes Mrs. Murchiston goes with me. Get up, Tubby!"

Tubby had to be urged incessantly; exertion was not loved by him. He would rather walk than trot; he would rather stand than walk; and he always had the appearance of being asleep—save when he was at his manger.

Ruth remembered that she had been warned not to go past "the gate with the green eyes" and she told Helen of her promise to Doctor Davison.

"Oh, splendid!" cried her chum. "I don't know anybody whom I like to call upon in Cheslow ahead of Doctor Davison. It's almost as good as having him come to see you when you're sick."

"But I don't think," Ruth objected, "that it's any fun to have any doctor come to see one on business."

"You don't half mind being ill when Doctor Davison calls," declared Helen, with unabated enthusiasm. "And when you call there! Well," concluded Helen, with a sigh of anticipation, "you'll soon know what that means. He's got a colored Mammy for cook who makes the most wonderful jumbles and cakes that you ever tasted—they about melt in pour mouth!"

Ruth soon had the opportunity of judging Mammy 'Liza's goodies for herself, for the doctor was at home, and the girls had scarcely become seated in his consultation room when a little colored girl with her wool "done" in innumerable pigtails, like tiny horns, and sticking out all over her brown head in every direction, came in with a tray on which was a plate piled high with fancy cakes and two tall glasses of yellow-gold beaten egg and milk with a dust of nutmeg floating upon the surface of each glassful.

"'Liza done sez as how yo'-all might be hongry aftah yo' ride," said the child, timidly, and then darted out of the room before Ruth and Helen could thank her.

They were munching the goodies when Doctor Davison came smilingly in.

"That's Mammy 'Liza all over," he said, shaking his head, but with his dark eyes twinkling. "I try to keep my young folk in good digestion and she is bound to make a patient of everybody who comes to see me. Cookies and cakes and sweets are what she believes girls live for; or else she is trying to make customers for my nasty drugs."

Doctor Davison seemed to have plenty of time to give to the society of young folk who called upon him. And he showed an interest in Ruth and her affairs which warmed our heroine's heart. He wanted to know how she got along at school, and if it was true that she was trying to "make" the High by the opening of the fall term.

"Not that I want any of my young folk to travel the road to

knowledge too steadily, or travel it when their bodily condition is not the best. But you are strong and well, Ruthie, and you can do a deal that other girls of your age would find irksome. I shall be proud if you prepare to enter the High at your age."

And this made Ruth feel more and more sure that Doctor Davison had taken interest enough in her career at school to supply the pretty frocks, one of which she was then wearing. But Aunt Alvirah had warned her that the frocks were to remain a mystery by the special request of the donor, and she could not ask the good old doctor anything about them. His interest in her progress seemed to infer that he expected Ruth to accomplish a great deal in her school, and the girl from the Red Mill determined not to disappoint him.

When Helen told Doctor Davison where else they intended to call, he nodded understandingly. "That is," he added, "Ruth will call on Mercy while you do your shopping, Miss Cameron. Oh, yes! that is the better plan. You know very well that Mercy Curtis won't want to see you, Helen."

"I don't know why not," said Helen, pouting. "I know she never treats anyone nicely, but I don't mind. If it does her good to do what Tom calls 'bully-ragging,' I can stand it as well as Ruth—better, perhaps."

"No," said the doctor, gravely. "I have told you before why you shouldn't call there. You have everything that Mercy can possibly desire. Comparisons with poor Mercy certainly are odious. Ruth, she knows, is not so fortunately placed in life as yourself. She is not so fortunately placed, indeed, as Mercy is. And Mercy is in an extremely nervous state just now, and I do not wish her to excite herself beyond reason."

"Well, I declare," exclaimed Helen, but good-naturedly after all. "I don't like to be told I'm not wanted anywhere. But if you say so, I'll not go with Ruth to the house."

Doctor Davison opened a new topic of conversation by asking after Tom.

"Oh, his head is all healed up—you can just barely see the scar," Helen declared. "And his arm is only a little tender. We think he got out of it very lucky indeed—thanks to Ruth here."

"Yes, thanks to Ruth," repeated the doctor, his eyes twinkling.

Ruth was "on pins and needles," as the saying is, for she very well remembered what the injured boy had murmured, in his half conscious state, when they brought him along the road on the stretcher. Had it been Jabez Potter who ran down Tom Cameron and forced him down the embankment with his motorcycle? This thought had been bobbing up in Ruth's mind ever since she had come to the Red Mill.

She had seen her uncle driving his team of mules in one of his reckless moods. She would never forget how the team tore down the long hill and was forced through the flood the day the Minturn dam had burst. Had Jabez Potter been driving through the dark road where Tom Cameron was hurt, in any such way as that, he would have run down a dozen cyclists without noticing them.

Fortunately Tom's injury had not been permanent. He was all right now. Ruth felt that she must be loyal to her uncle and say nothing about her own suspicions; but as long as the matter was discussed between Helen and Doctor Davison she was anxious. Therefore she hurried their departure from the kind physician's office, by rising and saying:

"I think we would better go, Helen. You know how slow Tubby is, and perhaps I can give the little Curtis girl some pleasure by calling on her."

"Without doubt she'll have pleasure," observed Helen, somewhat bitingly. "She is likely to scold and 'bullyrag' to her heart's content. You're such a meek thing that you'll let her."

"If that's what gives her pleasure, Helen," said Ruth, with a quiet smile, "why, I guess I can stand it for an hour."

Doctor Davison had risen likewise, and he went to the front door with them, his hand resting lightly on Ruth's shoulder.

"You have the right idea of it, Ruthie," he said. "Let Mercy take her pleasure in that way if it's all the pleasure she can get. But perhaps a better mind as well as a better body may come to the poor child in time." Then to Ruth he added, more personally: "Remember you have a friend in here behind the green lamps. Don't forget to come to him with any troubles you may have. Perhaps I do not look it, but I am something like a fairy godmother—I have a wonderful power of transmogrification. I can often turn dark clouds inside out and show you the silver on the other side."

"I believe that, Doctor Davison," she whispered, and squeezed his hand hard, running after Helen the next moment down the walk.

Alice B. Emerson

CHAPTER XVII

TORMENTING MERCY

After they had awakened Tubby and urged him into some-thing resembling a trot they got into Cheslow proper by degrees. By the light of the very sunshiny afternoon Ruth thought the town looked far prettier than any place she had ever seen. This side of the railroad the houses were mostly old-fashioned, and there were few stores. There were many lawns and pretty, old-time gardens, while the elms and maples met in green arches overhead so that many of the streets were like rustic tunnels, the sun sifting through the thick branches to make only a fine, lacework pattern upon the walks and driveway.

They crossed the railroad near the station and struck into Market Street. Ruth would not allow Helen to drive her directly to the Curtis cottage. She had remembered Doctor Davison's words, and she thought that perhaps Mercy Curtis might be looking from the window and see her visitor arrive in the pony cart. So she got down at the corner, promising to meet her friend at that spot in an hour.

She could see the pretty cottage belonging to the railroad station agent before she had walked far. Its garden on the side was already a bower. But the rustic arbor on which the grape vines were trained was not yet sufficiently covered to yield any shelter from the street; therefore Ruth did not expect to find it occupied.

Just before she reached the cottage, however, she saw two little girls ahead of her, hesitating on the walk. They were talking seriously together when Ruth approached within earshot, and she heard one say to the other:

"Now, she'll be there in the window. We mustn't notice her, no matter what she does or says. You know what mamma said."

The other child was sobbing softly. "But she made me, oh, such a face! And she chopped her teeth at me just as though she'd bite me! I think she's the very hatefulest thing—"

"Hush! she's greatly to be pitied," said the older sister, with an air and in a tone that showed she copied it from the "grown-ups" whom she had heard discussing poor Mercy Curtis.

"I wish we'd gone 'round the other way," complained the other child.

"Now, come on. You needn't look into the window and smile. I'll do that."

"No," said the little one, stubbornly. "I'll go by on the opposite side of the way. And you must come, too, Anna. She—she'd bite me if she could get the chance."

"Oh, well! Come on, little silly!" said her sister, and the two crossed over and Ruth, who watched them interestedly, saw them hurry by the cottage with scarcely a glance at the front windows.

Alice B. Emerson

But Ruth could see the outline of the lame girl's figure at one of the windows and she saw a lean fist shaken in the air at the two children going by. She could imagine the face Mercy Curtis "pulled," as well, and did not wonder that the two little ones took to their heels and ran away as fast as ever they could.

But, thus prepared for an unpleasant greeting from, the unfortunate and much to be pitied Mercy, Ruth smiled happily herself and waved her hand at the lame girl's window. Mercy saw her and, for a moment, was stricken with surprise so that she could neither greet her with frown or smile. She knew the girl from the Red Mill, although she had seen her so many weeks before; but Ruth ran into the yard and up the porch steps at the side of the house, and knocked at the door before the lame girl recovered from her amazement.

The motherly Mrs. Curtis came to the door and, the moment she saw who it was, received Ruth with open arms.

"You dear child! I am so glad you have come again. Did Doctor Davison tell you?" she whispered.

"He told me that Mercy would be glad to see me again; but I should have come before, as I promised, if I could have gotten in," Ruth said. "Will she see me?"

"She is not so well to-day," sighed the harassed mother. "This is one of her days of torment. I do not know how she will treat you, Ruth Fielding; but don't mind what she says to you, dear. Your being here will take her mind off her pain and off her own self."

Ruth laid aside her hat and coat and went into the sitting room. The crippled girl was in her wheel chair by the window. The instant Ruth entered she seized the wheels on either side and propelled the chair across the room in a sudden dash that threatened to run her visitor down. And her face was screwed up into such a mean look, and her eyes flashed so angrily, that Ruth was startled for a moment. But she stood her ground and instead of colliding with her, the nervous hands brought the chair to a sudden stop right before her.

"Thought you were going to be run down; didn't you?" snapped Mercy. "I'd ought to break your legs—you run on them so fine. Showing off; wasn't you?"

She was offended because Ruth had run so lightly into the cottage and the girl from the Red Mill made a decision there and then that she would never come in to see Mercy again saving at a sedate walk. But she laughed lightly, and said:

"Do you want me to come on crutches, Mercy? That wouldn't help you a bit."

She put out her hand to take the lame girl's, but Mercy struck it smartly with her own, then whirled her chair around and returned to her former position by the window. She handled the wheel chair with remarkable dexterity, and Ruth, following her and taking a neighboring chair said:

"How quick you are! You get around your room so nicely. I think that's fine."

"You do; do you?" snapped the cripple. "If you'd been tied to this chair like I have, you'd be quick, too. I suppose it's something for me to be grateful for; eh?"

"It must be a lot better than lying abed all the time," said Ruth, quietly.

"Oh, yes! I suppose so!" snapped Mercy. Her conversation was mostly made up of snaps and snarls. "Everybody tells me all about how happy I ought to be because I'm not worse off than I am. That's their tormenting ways—I know 'em! There!" she added, looking out of the window. "Here's another of those dratted young ones!"

Ruth glanced out, too. A lady was coming along the walk holding a little boy by the hand. Before they reached the cottage the little boy said something to his mother and then broke away from her hand and went to the other side of her, nearest the curb.

"There! he's hiding from me," said Mercy, bitterly.

The lady looked up and smiled pleasantly, but the cripple only returned her pleasant salutation with a cold nod. The child peeped out from around his mother's skirt.

"There! go along, you nasty little thing!" muttered Mercy. "See him trot on his little fat legs. I wish a dog would bite 'em!" It was useless, Ruth saw, to try and bring the cripple to a better mind. But she ignored her sallies at people who went by the window, and began to talk about the Red Mill and all that had happened to her since she had come to live with Uncle Jabez. Gradually she drew Mercy's attention from the street. She told about the flood, and how she, with Helen and Tom, had raced in the big automobile down the river road to warn the people that the water was coming. Mercy's eyes grew big with wonder and she listened with increasing interest.

"That's a nice place to live—that mill," the cripple finally admitted, grudgingly. "And it's right on the river, too!"

"I can look 'way up and down the river from my window the

first thing when I get up in the morning," Ruth said. "It's very pretty at sunrise. And then, the orchard and the fields are pretty. And I like to see the men ploughing and working the land. And the garden stuff is all coming up so pretty and green."

"I've got a garden, too. But it's not warm enough yet to plant many flower seeds," said Mercy.

"I suppose, when it comes warm, you can sit out in the arbor?"

"When the grape leaves get big enough to hide me—yes," said Mercy. "I don't go into the garden excepting in schooltime. Then the young ones aren't always running by and tormenting me," snapped the cripple, chopping off her speech at the end.

She was a self-tormentor. It was plain that the poor child made herself very miserable by believing that everybody possessing a strong back and lively legs felt his or her superiority to her and delighted in "showing off" before her. The girl of the Red Mill felt only pity for a sufferer possessing such an unfortunate disposition.

She tried to turn the conversation always into pleasant channels. She held Mercy's interest in the Red Mill and her life there. She told her of the broods of downy chicks that she cared for, and the butter-making, and the household tasks she was able to help Aunt Alviry about.

"And don't you go to school?" demanded Mercy.

"I am going now. I hope this spring and summer to prepare myself for entering the Cheslow High."

"And then you'll be in town every day?" said Mercy, with one of her occasional wistful looks.

"I hope to. I don't know how I will get here. But I mean to try. Miss Cramp says if I'll come two or three times a week this summer, after our school doses, that she will help me to prepare for the High School exams., so I can enter at the beginning of the fall term.

"I know Miss Cramp," said Mercy. "She lives on this street. You'll be so busy then that you'll never get in to see me at all, I suppose."

"Why, I can come much oftener," cried Ruth. "Of course I will."

If Mercy was pleased by this statement, she would not show it.

"I studied to enter High," she said, after a little silence. "But what's the use? I'll never go to school again. Reading books isn't any fun. Just studying, and studying, and studying doesn't get you anywhere."

"Why, I should think that would be nice," Ruth declared. "You've got so much chance to study. You see, you don't have to work around the house, or outside, and so you have all your time to devote to study. I should like that."

"Yah!" snarled Mercy, in her most unpleasant way. "That's what you say. I wish you were here to try it, and I could be out to the Red Mill." Then she paid more softly: "I'd like to see that mill and the river—and all the things you tell about."

"You wait!" cried Ruth. "I'll ask Uncle Jabez and Aunt Alviry. Maybe we can fix it so you could come out and see me. Wouldn't that be fine?"

"Yah!" snarled the cripple again. "I'll never get that far away from this old chair."

"Perhaps not; but you might bring the chair with you,", returned Ruth, unshaken. "Wait till vacation. I'll not give up the idea until I've seen if it can't be arranged."

That the thought pleased Mercy, the cripple could not deny. Her eyes shone and a warmth of unusual color appeared in her thin cheeks. Her mother came in with a tray of cakes and lemonade, and Mercy became quite pleasant as she did the honors. Having already eaten her fill at the doctor's, Ruth found it a little difficult to do justice to this collation; but she would not hurt Mercy's feelings by refusing.

The hour passed in more pleasant converse. The cripple's mind was evidently coaxed from its wrong and unhappy thoughts. When Ruth rose to leave, promising to come again as soon as she could get into town, Mercy was plainly softened.

"You just hate to come—I know you do!" she said, but she said it wistfully. "Everybody hates to come to see me. But I don't mind having you come as much as I do them. Oh, yes; you can come again if you will," and she gave Ruth her hand at parting.

Mrs. Curtis put her arms about the girl from the Red Mill and kissed her warmly at the door.

"Dear, dear!" said the cripple's mother, "how your own mother would have loved you, if she had lived until now. You are like sunshine in the house."

So, after waving her hand and smiling at the cripple in the window, Ruth went slowly back to the corner to meet Helen, and found herself wiping some tender tears from her eyes because of Mrs. Curtis's words.

CHAPTER XVIII

THE SPELLING BEE

In spite of the fact that the big girls at the district school, led by Julia Semple, whose father was the chairman of the board of trustees, had very little to say to Ruth Fielding, and shunned her almost altogether outside of the schoolroom, Ruth was glad of her chance to study and learn. She brought home no complaints to Aunt Alvirah regarding the treatment she received from the girls of her own class, and of course uncle Jabez never spoke to her about her schooling, nor she to him.

At school Ruth pleased Miss Cramp very much. She had gradually worked her way toward the top of the class—and this fact did not make her any more friends. For a new scholar to come into the school and show herself to be quicker and more thorough in her preparation for recitations than the older scholars naturally made some of the latter more than a little jealous.

Up to this time Ruth had never been to the big yellow house on the hill—"Overlook," as Mr. Macy Cameron called his estate. Always something had intervened when Ruth was about to go. But Helen and Tom insisted upon the very next Saturday following the girls' trip to Cheslow as the date

Alice B. Emerson

when Ruth must come to the big house to luncheon. The Camerons lived all of three miles from the Red Mill; otherwise Ruth would in all probability have been to her chum's home before.

Tom agreed to run down in the machine for his sister's guest at half-past eleven on the day in question, and Ruth hurried her tasks as much as possible so as to be all ready when he appeared in the big drab automobile. She even rose a little earlier, and the way she flew about the kitchen and porch at her usual Saturday morning tasks was, as Aunt Alvirah said, "a caution." But before Tom appeared Ruth saw, on one of her excursions into the yard, the old, dock-tailed, bony horse of Jasper Parloe drawing that gentleman in his rickety wagon up to the mill door.

"Hi, Jabe!" called Jasper, in his cracked voice. "Hi, Jabe! Here's a grindin' for ye. And for massy's sake don't take out a double toll as you us'ally do. Remember I'm a poor man—I ain't got lashin's of money like you to count ev'ry night of my life—he, he, he!"

The boy had appeared at the mill door first, and he stepped down and would have taken the bag of grain out of the wagon, had not the miller himself suddenly appeared and said, in his stern way:

"Let it be."

"Hi, Jabe!" cackled Jasper. "Don't be mean about it. He's younger than me, or you.

Let him shoulder the sack into the mill."

"The sack isn't coming into the mill," said Jabez, shortly.

"What? what?" cried Parloe. "You haven't retired from business; have you, miller? Ye ain't got so wealthy that ye ain't goin' to grind any more?"

"I grind for those whom it pleases me to grind for," said the miller, sternly.

"Then take in the bag, boy," said Jasper, still grinning.

But Mr. Potter waved the boy away, and stood looking at Jasper with folded arms and a heavy frown upon his face.

"Come, come, Jabe! you keep a mill. You grind for the public, you know," said Jasper.

"I grind no more for you," rejoined the miller. "I have told you so. Get you gone, Jasper Parloe."

"No," said the latter, obstinately. "I am going to have my meal."

"Not here," said the miller.

"Now, that's all nonsense, Jabe," exclaimed Jasper Parloe, wagging his head. "Ye know ye can't refuse me."

"I do refuse you."

"Then ye'll take the consequences, Jabe—ye'll take the consequences. Ye know very well if I say the word to Mr. Cameron—"

"Get away from here!" commanded Potter, interrupting. "I want nothing to do with you."

"You mean to dare me; do ye, Jabe?" demanded Jasper, with

an evil smile.

"I don't mean to have anything to do with a thief," growled the miller, and turning on his heel went back into the mill.

It was just then that Ruth spied the automobile coming down the road with Tom Cameron at the steering wheel. Ruth bobbed into the house in a hurry, with a single wave of her hand to Tom, for she was not yet quite ready. When she came down five minutes later, with a fresh ribbon in her hair and one of the new frocks that she had never worn before looking its very trimmest, Jasper Parloe had alighted from his ramshackle wagon and was talking with Tom, who still sat in the automobile.

And as Ruth stood in the porch a moment, while Aunt Alvirah proudly looked her over to see that she was all right, the girl saw by the expression on Tom's face that whatever Parloe talked about was not pleasing the lad in the least.

She saw, too, that Tom pulled something from his pocket hastily and thrust it into Parloe's hand. The old man chuckled slily, said something else to the boy, and then turned away and climbed into his wagon again. He drove away as Ruth ran down the path to the waiting auto.

"Hullo, Tom!" she cried. "I told you I wouldn't keep you waiting long."

"How-do, Ruth," he returned; but it must be confessed that he was not as bright and smiling as usual, and he looked away from Ruth and after Parloe the next moment.

As the girl reached the machine Uncle Jabez came to the mill door again. He observed Ruth about to get in and he came down the steps and strode toward the Cameron automobile.

Jasper Parloe had clucked to his old nag and was now rattling away from the place.

"Where are you going, Ruth?" the miller demanded, sternly eyeing Tom Cameron, and without returning the lad's polite greeting.

"She is going up to our house to lunch with my sister, Mr. Potter," Tom hastened to say before Ruth could reply.

"She will do nothing of the kind," said Uncle Jabez, shortly. "Ruth, go back to the house and help your Aunt Alvirah. You are going about too much and leaving your aunt to do everything."

This was not so, and Ruth knew very well that her uncle knew it was not so. She flushed and hesitated, and he said:

"Do you hear me? I expect to be obeyed if you remain here at the Red Mill. Just because I lay few commands upon you, is no reason why you should consider it the part of wisdom to be disobedient when I do give an order."

"Oh, Uncle! do let me go," begged Ruth, fairly crying. "Helen has been so kind to me—and Aunt Alvirah did not suppose you would object. They come here—"

"But I do not propose that they shall come here any more," declared Uncle Jabez, in the same stern tone. "You can drive on, young man. The less I see of any of you Camerons the better I shall like it."

"But, Mr. Potter—" began Tom.

The old man raised his hand and stopped him.

Alice B. Emerson

"I won't hear any talk about it. I know just how much these Camerons have done for you," he said to Ruth. "They've done enough—altogether too much. We will stop this intimacy right here and now. At least, you will not go to their house, Ruth. Do as I tell you—go in to your Aunt Alviry."

Then, as the weeping girl turned away, she heard him say, even more harshly than he had spoken to her: "I don't want anything to do with people who are hand and glove with that Jasper Parloe. He's a thief—a bigger thief, perhaps, than people generally know. At least, he's cost me enough. Now, you drive on and don't let me see you or your sister about here again."

He turned on his heel and went back to the mill without giving Tom time to say a word. The boy, angry enough, it was evident from his expression of countenance, hesitated several minutes after the miller was gone. Once he arose, as though he would get out of the car and follow Jabez into the mill. But finally he started the engine, turned the car, and drove slowly away.

This was a dreadful day indeed for the girl of the Red Mill. Never in her life had she been so hurt—never had she felt herself so ill-used since coming to this place to live. Uncle Jabez had never been really kind to her; but aside from the matter of the loss of her trunk he had never before been actually cruel.

He could have selected no way that would have hurt her more keenly. To refuse to let her go to see the girl she loved—her only close friend and playmate! And to refuse to allow Helen and Tom to come here to see her! This intimacy was all (and Ruth admitted it now, in a torrent of tears, as she lay upon her little bed) that made life at the Red Mill endurable. Had she not met Helen and found her such a dear girl and so kind a companion, Ruth told herself now that she never could have borne the dull existence of this house.

She heard Aunt Alvirah's halting step upon the stair and before the old woman reached the top of the flight, Ruth plainly heard her moaning to herself: "Oh, my back! and oh, my bones!" Thus groaning and halting, Aunt Alvirah came to Ruth's door and pushed it open.

"Oh, deary, deary, me!" she whispered, limping into the room. "Don't-ee cry no more, poor lamb. Old Aunt Alviry knows jest how it hurts—she wishes she could bear it for ye! Now, now, my pretty creetur—don't-ee take on so. Things will turn out all right yet. Don't lose hope."

She had reached the bed ere this and had gathered the sobbing girl into her arms. She sat upon the side of the bed and rocked Ruth to and fro, with her arms about her. She did not say much more, but her unspoken sympathy was wonderfully comforting.

Aunt Alvirah did not criticise Uncle Jabez's course. She never did. But she gave Ruth in her sorrow all the sympathy of which her great nature was capable. She seemed to understand just how the girl felt, without a spoken word on her part. She did not seek to explain the miller's reason for acting as he did. Perhaps she had less idea than had Ruth why Jabez Potter should have taken such a violent dislike to the Camerons.

For Ruth half believed that she held the key to that mystery. When she came to think it over afterward she put what she had heard between the two old men—Jabez and Parloe—down at the brook, with what had occurred at the mill just before Tom Cameron had come in sight; and putting these two incidents together and remembering that Jasper Parloe had overheard Tom in his delirium accuse the miller of being the cause of his injury, Ruth was pretty sure that in that combination of circumstances was the true explanation of Uncle Jabez's cruel decision.

Ruth was not the girl to lie on her bed and weep for long. She was sensible enough to know very well that such a display of disappointment and sorrow would not better the circumstances. While she remained at the Red Mill she must obey Uncle Jabez, and his decisions could not be controverted. She had never won a place near enough to the miller's real nature to coax him, or to reason with him regarding this gruff decision he had made. She had to make up her mind that, unless something unexpected happened to change Uncle Jabez, she was cut off from much future association with her dear chum, Helen Cameron.

She got up in a little while, bathed her face and eyes, and kissed Aunt Alvirah warmly.

"You are a dear!" she declared, hugging the little old woman. "Come! I won't cry any more. I'll come down stairs with you, Auntie, and help get dinner."

But Ruth could eat none herself. She did not feel as though she could even sit at the table with Uncle Jabez that noon, and remained outside while the miller ate. He never remarked upon her absence, or paid her the least attention. Oh, how heartily Ruth wished now that she had never come away from Darrowtown and had never seen the Red Mill.

The next Monday morning the rural mail carrier brought her a long letter from Helen. Uncle Jabez had not said anything against a correspondence; indeed, Ruth did not consider that he had more than refused to have the Camerons come to see her or she to return their visits. If she met them on the road, or away from the house, she did not consider that it would be disobeying Uncle Jabez to associate with Helen and Tom.

This letter from Helen was very bitter against the miller and wildly proposed that Ruth should run away from the Red Mill and come to Overlook to live. She declared that her papa would not object—indeed, that everybody would warmly welcome the appearance of Ruth Fielding "even if she came like a tramp "; and that Tom would linger about the Red Mill for an hour or two every evening so that Ruth could slip out and communicate with her friends, or could be helped away if she wanted to leave without the miller's permission.

But Ruth, coming now to consider her situation more dispassionately, simply wrote a loving letter in reply to Helen's, entrusting it to the post, and went on upon her usual way, helping Aunt Alviry, going to school, and studying harder than ever. She missed Helen's companionship vastly; she often wet her pillow with tears at night (and that was not like Ruth) and felt very miserable indeed at times.

But school and its routine took up a deal of the girl's thought. Her studies confined her more and more as the end of the term approached. And in addition to the extra work assigned the girl at the Red Mill by Miss Cramp, there was a special study which Ruth wished to excel in. Miss Cramp was old-fashioned enough to believe that spelling was the very best training for the mind and the memory and that it was a positive crime for any child to grow up to be a slovenly speller. Four times a year Miss Cramp held an old-fashioned "spelling-bee" at the schoolhouse, on designated Friday evenings; and now came the last of the four for this school year.

Ruth had never been an extra good speller, but because her

Alice B. Emerson

kind teacher was so insistent upon the point, the girl from the Red Mill put forth special efforts to please Miss Cramp in this particular. She had given much spare time to the study of the spelling book, and particularly did she devote herself to that study now that she hadn't her chum to associate with.

The spelling-bees were attended by the parents of the pupils and all the neighbors thereabout, and Helen wrote that she and Tom were going to attend on the evening in question and that Tom said he hoped to see Ruth "just eat up those other girls" when it came to spelling. But Ruth Fielding much doubted her cannibalistic ability in this line. Julia Semple had borne off the honors on two occasions during the winter, and her particular friend Rosa Ball, had won the odd trial. Now it was generally considered that the final spelling-bee would be the occasion of a personal trial of strength between the two friendly rivals. Either Julia or Rosa must win.

But Ruth was the kind of a person who, in attempting a thing, did her very best to accomplish it. She had given some time and thought to the spelling book. She was not likely to "go down" before any easy, or well-known word. Indeed, she believed herself letter perfect in the very hardest page of the spelling-book some time before the fateful evening.

"Oh, perhaps you think you know them all, Ruth Fielding!" exclaimed one of the little girls one day when the spelling-bee was being discussed at recess. "But Miss Cramp doesn't stick to the speller. You just wait till she tackles the dictionary."

"The dictionary!" cried Ruth.

"That's what Miss Cramp does," the child assured her. "If she can't spell them down out of the speller, she begins at the beginning of the dictionary and gives words out until she finds one that floors them all. You wait and see!"

So Ruth thought it would do no harm to study the dictionary a little, and taking her cue from what the little girls said, she remained in between sessions and began with "aperse," committing to memory as well as she could those words that looked to be "puzzlers." Before the day of the spelling-bee she believed that, if Miss Cramp didn't go beyond the first letter of the alphabet, she would be fairly well grounded in the words as they came in rotation.

Ruth knew that every other pupil in the school would have friends in the audience that evening save herself. She wished that Aunt Alvirah could have attended the spelling-bee; but of course her back and her bones precluded her walking so far, and neither of them dared ask Uncle Jabez to hitch up and take them to the schoolhouse in his wagon.

The schoolhouse was crowded, all the extra seats that could be provided were arranged in rows, and, it being a mild evening, the men and bigger boys stood outside the open windows. There was a great bustle and whispering until Miss Cramp's tinkling bell called the audience as well as the pupils to order.

The scholars took their places according to their class standing in a long row around the room. As one was spelled down he or she took a seat again, and so the class was rapidly thinned out, for many of the little folk missed on the very easiest words in the speller. Ruth stood within ten pupils of the head of the line at the beginning and when the spelling began she had an encouraging smile and nod from Helen, who, with her brother, sat where they could see the girl from the Red Mill Ruth determined to do her best.

CHAPTER XIX

THE STING OF POVERTY

At first Miss Cramp's "giving out" of the words was like repeated volleys of small-arms in this orthographical battle. Every pupil well knew the pages of two-syllable words beginning, "baker, maker, poker, broker, quaker, shaker" and even the boys rattled these off, grinning the while in a most sheepish fashion at their elder brothers or their women-folk, who beamed in pride upon them until such lists as "food, soup, meat, bread, dough, butter" bowled over the more shaky ones.

The first failures (and usually upon comparatively easy words) were greeted with some laughter, and the ridiculed spellers sought their seats with hanging heads. By and by, however, the failures were not all at the bottom of the class; here and there such lists as "inane, profane, humane, insane, mundane, urbane," or, "staid, unlaid, mermaid, prayed, weighed, portrayed" began to pick out uncertain ones the entire length of the line.

Miss Cramp shot out word after word, her spectacles gleaming and her eyes twinkling. The grim little smile upon her lips when one big girl above Ruth went down before "forswear," spelling it with an extra "e," showed that the teacher considered the miss deserved to fail because of her heedlessness. Then, when she reached the list ending in "ay, ey and eigh" they fell like ripe huckleberries all down the line. "Inveigh" dropped so many that it was indeed a massacre, and some of the nervous spellers got together such weird combinations of letters to represent that single word that the audience was soon in a very hilarious state.

"Move up," commanded Miss Cramp to the pupils left standing, and there was a great clumping of feet as the line closed up. Not more than two dozen were standing by this time, and half an hour had not passed. But after that it was another story. The good spellers remained. They spelled carefully and quietly and a hush fell upon the whole room as Miss Cramp gave out the words with less haste and more precision.

The "seeds," as all the children called the puzzling list, floored two, and several of the best spellers had to think carefully while the list was being given out: "proceed, succeed, exceed, accede, secede, recede, impede, precede, concede, antecede, intercede, supersede." Fortunately Ruth, who now kept her eyes upon Miss Cramp's face, spelled carefully and correctly, without any sign of hesitancy. The match went on then, for page after page, without a pupil failing. Perhaps there was hesitation at times, but Miss Cramp gave any deserving scholar ample time.

Page after page of the spelling-book was turned. That tricksey little list of "goblin, problem, conduct, rocket, pontiff, compact, prospect, ostrich" finally left but three scholars between Ruth and Julia at the head of the class. One of these was Oliver Shortsleeves, a French Canadian lad whose parents had Anglicised their name when they came down into New York State. He was as sharp as could be and he had pushed Julia Semple and Rosa Ball hard before in the spelling matches. But he was the only boy left standing within the next few minutes, and again the pupils moved up. There were but fifteen of them. Rosa Ball came next to Ruth, below her, and the girl from the Red Mill knew very well that Miss Ball would only be too delighted to spell her, Ruth, down.

Indeed, when Ruth waited a moment before spelling" seraglio," Rosa in her haste blurted out the word, and Julia smiled and there was a little rustle of expectancy. It was evident that many of the scholars, as well as the audience, thought Ruth had failed.

"Wait!" exclaimed Miss Cramp, sharply. "Did I pass that word to you, Rosa?"

"No, ma'am; but I thought

"Never mind what you thought. You know the rule well enough," said Miss Cramp. "That will be your word, and I will give Ruth Fielding another. Spell 'seraglio' again, Rosa."

"'S e r a l g i o'," spelled Rosa.

"I thought in your haste to get ahead of Ruth you spelled it wrongly, Rosa," said Miss Cramp, calmly. "You may go down. Next—'Seraglio.'"

Miss Ball went down in tears—angry tears—but there was not much sympathy shown her by the audience, and little by her fellow-pupils. It was soon seen that there was some sort of rivalry between Ruth and Julia, and that the girl from the Red Mill had not been treated fairly.

Oliver Shortsleeves became sadly twisted up after hearing those immediately before him spell in succession "schooner, tetrarch, pibroch and anarchy" and tried to spell "architrave" with so many letters that he would have needed no more to have spelled it twice over. So Ruth then became fourth in the line. She continued to spell carefully and serenely. Nothing disturbed her poise, for she neither looked around the room nor gave heed to anything that went on save Miss Cramp's distinctly uttered words,

On and on went the steady voice of Miss Cramp. She bowled over one pupil with "microcosm," another the next minute with "metonymy "; "nymphean" and "naphtha" sent two more to their seats; while the silent "m" in "mnemonics" cut a most fearful swath in the remainder, so that after the smoke of that bomb was dissipated only Julia, Ruth, and two others stood of all the class.

Julia Semple had darted many angry glances et Ruth since the cutting down of her friend, Rosa Ball, and her flaunting of the girl from the Red Mill, and her scornful looks, might easily have disturbed Ruth had the latter not been wise enough to keep her own gaze fixed upon the teacher.

Helen and Tom were delighted and plainly showed their enjoyment of Ruth's success. Now, as the situation became more strained, the audience applauded when one of the spellers overcame a more than ordinarily difficult word. So that when the girl next to Ruth missed "tergiversation" and it passed to the girl from the Red Mill, who spelled it without hesitation, and correctly, Helen applauded softly, while Tom audibly exclaimed: "Good for Ruthie!"

This did not make Julia Semple any more pleasant. She actually looked across at Helen and Tom and scowled at them. It had already begun to be whispered about the room that the match was easily Julia's—that she was sure to win; and Mr. Semple, the chairman of the trustees, who sat on the

Alice B. Emerson

platform with the teacher, looked very well satisfied indeed.

But Miss Cramp had come down now to the final words in the speller—down to "zenith" and "zoology." And still there were three standing. Miss Cramp looked for a moment as though she would like to announce the match a tie between the trio, for it was plain there would be hard feelings engendered among some of the audience, as well as the pupils, if the match continued. Her custom had been, however, to go on to the bitter end—to spell down the very last one, and she could not easily make a change in her method now.

A general sigh and whispering went around when she was seen to reach for the academic dictionary which was always the foundation of the tower of books upon the northeast corner of Miss Cramp's desk. She opened the volume and shot out the word: "Aperse."

The girl standing between Ruth and Julia staggered along until they reached "abstinence "; she put an "e" instead of an "i" in the middle syllable, and went down. But the audience applauded her. Julia Semple began to hesitate now. The end was near. Perhaps she had never taken the time to follow down the rows of words in the dictionary. At "acalycal" she stumbled, started twice, then stopped and asked to have it repeated.

"'Acalycal,'" said Miss Cramp, steadily.

"'A c a l l y c a l,'" stammered Julia.

"Wrong," said Miss Cramp, dispassionately.

"Next. 'Acalycal'?"

Ruth spelled it with two 'l's' only and Miss Cramp looked

up quickly.

"Right," she said. "You may step down, Julia. It has been our custom to keep on until the winner is spelled down, too. Next word, Ruth: 'acalycine.'"

But there was such a buzz of comment that Miss Cramp looked up again. Julia Semple had seemed half stunned for the moment. Then she wheeled on Ruth and said, in a sharp whisper:

"I saw that Cameron girl spell it for you! She's been helping you all the time! Everybody knows she's patronizing and helping you. Why, you're wearing her old, cast-off clothes. You've got one of her dresses on now! Pauper!"

Ruth started back, her face turned red, then white, as though she had been struck. The smarting tears started to her eyes, and blinded her.

"Julia! take your seat instantly!" said Miss Cramp, more sharply. "Ruth! spell 'acalycine.'"

But Ruth could not open her lips. Had she done so she would have burst into tears. And she could not have spelled the word right—nor any other word right—at that moment. She merely shook her head and followed Julia to her seat, stumblingly, while a dead silence fell upon the room.

CHAPTER XX

UNCLE JABEZ IS MYSTERIOUS

Miss Cramp was in the habit of calling upon some trustee to speak at the close of the exercises—usually Mr. Semple—and then there was a little social time before the assemblage broke up. But the frown on the chairman's face did not suggest that that gentleman had anything very jovial to say at the moment, and the teacher closed the exercises herself in a few words that were not at all personal to the winner of the spelling-match.

When the stir of people moving about aroused Ruth, her only thought was to get away from the schoolhouse. Perhaps not more than two dozen people had distinctly heard what Julia so cruelly said to her; but it seemed to the girl from the Red Mill as though everybody in that throng knew that she was a charity child—that, as Julia said, the very frock she had on belonged to somebody else.

And to Helen! She had never for a moment suspected that Helen had been the donor of the three frocks. Of course everybody in the neighborhood had known all the time that she was wearing Helen's cast-off clothing. Everybody but Ruth herself would have recognized the dresses; she had been in the neighborhood so short a time that, of course, she was not very well acquainted with Helen's wardrobe.

At the moment she could not feel thankful to her chum. She could only remember Julia's cutting words, and feel the sting to her pride that she should have shown herself before all beholders the recipient of her friend's alms.

Nobody spoke to her as she glided through the moving crowd and reached the door. Miss Cramp was delayed in getting to her; Helen and Tom did not see her go, for they were across the room and farthest from the door. And so she reached the exit and slipped out.

The men and boys from outside thronged the tiny anteroom and the steps. As she pushed through them one man said:

"Why, here's the smart leetle gal that took Semple's gal down a peg—eh? She'd oughter have a prize for that, that's what she ought!"

But Ruth could not reply to this, although she knew it was meant kindly. She went out into the darkness. There were many horses hitched about the schoolhouse, but she reached the clear road in safety and ran toward the Red Mill.

The girl came to the mill and went quietly into the kitchen. She had got the best of her tears now, but Aunt Alviry's bright eyes discovered at once that she was unhappy. Uncle Jabez did not even raise his eyes when she came in.

"What is the matter with my pretty leetle creetur?" whispered the old woman, creeping close to Ruth.

"Nothing is the matter now," returned Ruth, in the same low tone.

Alice B. Emerson

"Didn't you do well?" asked the old woman, wistfully.

"I won the spelling match," replied Ruth. "I stood up longer than anybody else."

"Is that so!" exclaimed Aunt Alvirah, with pride. "I told ye so, Ruthie. And ye beat that Semple gal?"

"She was the last one to fail before me," Ruth returned.

"Well, well! D'ye hear that, Jabez? Our Ruth won the spellin'-match."

The miller did not raise his head from his accounts; only grunted and nodded.

"But something went wrong wi' ye, deary?" persisted Aunt Alvirah, watching Ruth's face closely.

"Oh, Auntie! why didn't you tell me that Helen gave me the frocks?"

"Deary, deary, me!" ejaculated Aunt Alvirah. "How did you know?"

"Julia Semple told me—she told me before everybody!" gasped Ruth, fighting hard to keep back the tears. "She called me a pauper! She called it out before them all, and said that I wore Helen's cast-off clothes!"

"The mean thing!" said Aunt Alvirah, with more sharpness then she usually expressed. "Isn't that jest like the Semples? They're all that way. Got mad with you because you beat her at spelling; eh?"

"Yes. But she has known it right along, of course."

"Deary me!" said Aunt Alvirah. "Nobody supposed them frocks would be reckernized—least of all Helen. She meant it kindly, Ruthie. It was kindly meant,"

"I wish I'd worn my old black dress to rags!" cried Ruth, who was too hurt to be sensible or just. "I suppose Helen meant it kindly. And you did what you thought was right, Auntie. But all the girls have turned up their noses at me—"

"Let 'em stay turned up—what do you care?" suddenly growled Uncle Jabez.

For the moment Ruth had forgotten his presence and she and Aunt Alvirah had been talking more loudly. They both fell suddenly silent and stared at him.

"Are ye too proud to wear dresses that's give to ye?" demanded Uncle Jabez. "Ye ain't too proud to take food and shelter from me. And I'm a poorer man than Macy Cameron an' less able to give."

The tone and the words were both cruel—or seemed to be to Ruth's mind. But she said, bravely:

"People know that you're my uncle—"

"I was yer mother's uncle; that's all. The relationship ain't much," declared Uncle Jabez.

"Jabez," said the little old woman, solemnly, "you've been a good friend to me—ye've borne with me in sickness and in weakness. Ye took me from the a'mshouse when I didn't have a penny to my name and nobody else to turn to, it seemed. I've tried ter do for ye faithfully. But I ain't done my duty by you no more than this child here has since she's come here to the Red Mill. You know that well yourself, too.

Don't blame the pretty leetle creetur for havin' the nateral vanity that all young things hez. Remember, Jabez, that it was through you that she has had to accept clothing from outsiders."

"Through me?" growled the miller, raising his countenance and scowling at the brave old woman—for it took courage for Aunt Alvirah to speak to him in this way.

"Helen Cam'ron wouldn't have been called on to give Ruthie her frocks which she only wore last year, and outgrew, if you hadn't lost Ruthie's trunk. Ye know that, Jabez," urged Aunt Alvirah.

"I s'pose I'm never to hear the last of that!" stormed the miller.

"You are still to hear the first word from Ruthie about it, Jabez," admonished his housekeeper.

"Well!"

"Well," repeated Aunt Alvirah, still speaking quietly but earnestly. "You know it ain't my way to interfere in your affairs, Jabez. But right is right. It was you lost Ruthie's trunk. I never knew ye ter be dishonest—"

"What's that?" gasped Mr. Potter, the red mantling his gray cheek dully.

"I never knew ye ter do a dishonest thing afore, Jabez," pursued Aunt Alvirah, with her voice shaking now. "But it's dishonest for ye to never even perpose ter make good what ye lost. If you'd lost a sack of grain for a neighbor ye'd made it up to him; wouldn't ye?"

"What's thet gotter do with a lot of foolish fal-lals an' rigamagigs belonging to a gal that I've taken in—"

"To help us. And she does help us," declared the old woman, quickly. "She more'n airns her keep, Jabez. Ye know she does."

"Well!" grunted the miller again, but he actually looked somewhat abashed and dropped his gaze to the ledger.

"Well, then, Jabez Potter," said the old housekeeper, "you think it over—think it over, Jabez. And as sure as my name's Alviry Boggs, if you do think it over, something will come of it!"

This seemed like a rather mysterious saying, and there seemed to be nothing for the miller to observe in answer to it. Ruth had ere this dried her eyes and it was soon bedtime. It is a long time from Friday night to Monday morning—especially to young folk. The hurt that Ruth had felt over Julia Semple's unkind words had lost its keenness in Ruth's mind ere school began again. So Ruth took up her school duties quite as usual, wearing one of the pretty frocks in which, however, she could no longer take such pride and delight.

There was really nothing for her to do but wear them. She realized that. She felt, however, that whenever any girl looked at her she remembered that it was Helen Cameron's cast-off dress she wore; so she was glad that the big girls were no more friendly than before and that they seldom looked at her.

Besides, all the school was very busy now. In a fortnight would came graduation. About all Ruth heard at recess and between sessions, even among the smaller girls, was the discussion of what they were to wear on the last day of the term. It was a great day at this school, and Miss Cramp was to graduate from her care seven pupils—four girls and three boys—all of whom would go to the Cheslow High the coming year. Ruth would not be ready to graduate; but before fall, if she was faithful to the tasks Miss Cramp set her, that kind teacher assured the girl from the Red Mill that she would be able to enter the higher school with this graduating class.

All the older girls and many of the others were to wear white. Miss Cramp approved of this, for even a simple white dress would look pretty and nice and was within the means of most of the girl pupils. Nobody asked Ruth what she would wear; and she was glad of that, for she knew that she had no choice but to don the shabby black cloth frock she had worn at first, or one of the "charity" frocks.

In this first week after the spelling-bee she did not see Helen or Tom, and only received a brief note from Helen which she tried to answer with her usual cheerfulness. Helen and Tom were going to the city for a few days, therefore Ruth was not likely to see either until the end of the term.

At the Red Mill matters went much the same as usual. If Uncle Jabez had taken to heart anything that Aunt Alvirah had said, he did not show it. He was as moody as ever and spoke no more to Ruth than before. But once or twice the girl found him looking at her with a puzzled frown which she did not understand.

On Saturday, however, at dinner, Mr. Potter said: "Alviry, if the gal has got her work done she can go to town with me this afternoon."

Ruth shrank a little and looked appealingly at the old

woman. But Aunt Alvirah would not or did not, understand Ruth's pleading, and said, briskly:

"She shall be ready when you've shaved and Ben's harnessed the mules, Jabez."

"Oh, Auntie!" whispered Ruth, when the miller had gone out, "I don't want to go with him! I don't really!"

"Now, don't say that, child," said Aunt Alvirah. "Don't do nothing to make him feel that ye air afraid of him. Go 'long. Ye can call on that leetle lame gal ye was tellin' us about while Jabez does his errands. Now hurry, deary."

Ruth felt quite confused by this. It seemed that there must be some private understanding between Aunt Alvirah and the miller. She went slowly and changed her frock. The old lady, crying up the stairway after her, advised her to look her smartest—so as to please Jabez, forsooth! Indeed, she finally hobbled up stairs, with many ejaculations of "Oh, my back and oh, my bones!" for the purpose of satisfying herself that Ruth was as nicely dressed as she could be.

And Uncle Jabez—or no other man—need have been ashamed of the appearance of Ruth Fielding when the mules came around hitched to the heavy farm-wagon which Mr. Potter usually drove. It was piled high with bags of flour and meal, which he proposed to exchange at the Cheslow stores for such supplies as he might need. The load seemed heavier than usual this day.

It was not a bad wagon to ride in, though dusty; for there was a spring seat and over it a new hood to shield the riders from the sun. Ruth followed Uncle Jabez out of the house and climbed up over the wheel and into the seat when he nodded for her to do so. He followed her, took up the reins, and the

Alice B. Emerson

boy, Ben, stood away from the mules' heads.

Aunt Alvirah stood on the porch and waved her apron at Ruth every time the girl turned around, until the wagon had crossed the bridge and was way up the long hill on the Cheslow road. It was a delightful June afternoon and had Ruth been traversing this pleasant highway in almost any other way, she would have enjoyed the ride mightily.

CHAPTER XXI

THE END OF THE TERM

But the companionship of the grim and glum proprietor of the Red Mill was not conducive—in Ruth's case, at least—to any feeling of pleasure. Uncle Jabez seemed about to speak to her a dozen times before they were out of sight of the mill; but every time Ruth turned toward him, half expecting to be addressed, his lips were grimly set and he was looking straight ahead over the mules' ears.

It is doubtful if Uncle Jabez saw anything of the beauty of the day or the variety of the landscape. Looking as he did he could not have observed by his eyes of flesh much but the brown ribbon of road before them, for miles. And it is doubtful if, spiritually, he appreciated much of the beauty of the June day. The mules toiled up the long hill, straining in their collars; but they began to trot upon the other side of the ridge and the five miles to Cheslow were covered in a comparatively short time.

Finally, when Uncle Jabez drew up before one of the largest stores, she felt that she must break the awful silence. And stumblingly she preferred her request:

"If you are going to be some time trading, Uncle Jabez, can't

I go down to call on Mercy Curtis? I can come here again and meet you at any time you say."

"Who's that? Sam Curtis' gal—the cripple?" asked Uncle Jabez, shortly.

"Yes, sir. She likes to have me come and see her."

"Can't you find nothing more interestin' to do when ye come to town than go to see a sick gal?" was the miller's surprising inquiry.

"I—I promised to call on her if I could whenever I was in town. She really likes to have me come," explained Ruth.

"Well, you can go," grunted Uncle Jabez. "I'll stop there for ye when I'm done tradin'."

He had already climbed down from the high seat. Ruth came lightly down after him and he actually turned and jumped her over the wheel so that her dress should not be soiled. Then, suddenly, he said:

"Wait. I want you to go into this store with me first."

He turned away abruptly, so that Ruth could not see what his countenance expressed. He carefully tied his mules to a hitching post and then stumped into the store without again glancing in her direction. Ruth followed him timidly.

It was a big store with many departments, and on one side were dry goods and clothing, where the clerks were women, or young girls, while the groceries, provisions, hardware and agricultural tools were displayed upon the other side of the long room. Uncle Jabez strode straight to the first woman he saw who was disengaged.

"This girl wants a dress to wear to the school graduating," he said, in his harsh voice. "It must be white. Let her pick out the goods, all the fal-lals that go with it, and a pattern to make it by. Ye understand?"

"Yes, sir," said the woman, smiling.

"You know me?" asked Uncle Jabez. "Yes? Then send the bill to the other side of the store and I'll pay it when I sell my meal and flour." Then to the astounded Ruth he said: "I'll come to Sam Curtis' for you when I'm done. See you don't keep me waiting."

He wheeled and strode away before Ruth could find her voice. She was so amazed that she actually felt faint She could not understand it. A white dress! And she to make her choice alone, without regard to material, or price! She could have been no more stunned had Uncle Jabez suddenly run mad and been caught by the authorities and sent to an asylum.

But the shop woman awoke her, having asked her twice what kind of white goods she wanted to see. The repeated query brought Ruth to her senses. She put the astonishing fact that Uncle Jabez had done this, behind her, and remembered at once the importance of the task before her.

She had not listened to the talk of the other girls at school for nothing. She knew just what was the most popular fabric that season for simple white dresses that could be "done up" when soiled. She had even found the style of a dress she liked in a fashion magazine that one of the girls had had at school. Ruth was self-posessed at once. She went about her shopping as carefully and with as little haste as though she had been buying for herself for years; whereas this was the very first frock that she had ever been allowed to have the

Alice B. Emerson

choice of.

There were costlier goods, and some of the girls of the graduating class were to have them; but Ruth chose something so durable and at so low a price that she hoped Uncle Jabez would not be sorry for his generosity. She saw the goods, and lace, and buttons, and all the rest, made up into a neat package and sent across to the other counter with the bill, and then went out of the store and up Market Street toward the railroad.

She saw Uncle Jabez nowhere, or she would have run to him to thank him for the present. And she had been in Mercy Curtis' front window for quite an hour before the mules turned the corner into the street and the wagon rattled up to the house and stopped.

"And is that ugly old man your uncle?" demanded Mercy, who had been less crusty and exacting herself on this occasion.

"That is Uncle Jabez;" admitted Ruth, hastening to put on her hat.

"He is an ugly one; isn't he? I'd like to know him, I would," declared the odd child. "He ain't one that's always smirking and smiling, I bet you!"

"He isn't given much to smiling, I must admit," laughed Ruth, stooping to kiss the crippled girl.

"There! Go along with you," said Mercy, sharply. "You tell that ugly, dusty man—Dusty Miller, that's what he is—that I'm coming out to the Red Mill, whether he wants me to or not."

And when Ruth got out upon the street Mercy had her window open and cried through the opening, shaking her little fist the while:

"Remember! You tell Dusty Miller what I told you! I'm coming out there."

"What's the matter with that young one?" growled Uncle Jabez, as Ruth climbed aboard and the mules started at a trot before she was really seated beside him.

Ruth told him, smiling, that Mercy had taken a fancy to his looks, and a fancy, too, to the Red Mill from her description of it. "She wants very much to come out there this summer—if she can be moved that far."

Then Ruth tried to thank the miller for the frock—which bundle she saw carefully placed among the other packages in the body of the wagon—but Uncle Jabez listened very grumpily to her broken words.

"I don't know how to thank you, sir; for of all the things I wanted most, I believe this is the very first thing," Ruth said, stumblingly. "I really don't know how to thank you."

"Don't try, then," he growled, but without looking at her. "I reckon you can thank Alviry Boggs as much as anybody. She says I owed it to you."

"Oh, Uncle—"

"There, there! I don't wanter hear no more about it," declared the miller. But after they had rattled on for a while in silence, he said, pursuing the former topic: "There ain't no reason, I s'pose, why that gal can't come out an' see you bimeby, if you want her to."

Alice B. Emerson

"Oh, thank you, Uncle Jabez!" cried Ruth, feeling as though something very strange indeed must have happened to the miller to make him so agreeable. And she tried to be chatty and pleasant with him for the rest of the way home. But Uncle Jabez was short on conversation—he seemed to have hoarded that up, too, and was unable to get at his stores of small-talk. Most of his observations were mere grunts and nods, and that evening he was just as glum and silent as ever over his money and accounts.

Miss 'Cretia Lock arrived early on Monday morning and when Ruth came home from school in the afternoon the wonderful dress was cut out. They made it in two days and Aunt Alvirah washed and starched and ironed it herself and it was ready for appearance on the last Friday afternoon of the term, when the district school held its graduating exercises.

CHAPTER XXII

MERCY

Ruth felt that she was not very successful at Miss Cramp's school. Not that she had fallen behind in her studies, or failed to please her kind instructor; but among the pupils of the upper grade she was all but unconsidered. Perhaps, had time been given her, Ruth might have won her way with some of the fairer-minded girls; but in the few short weeks she had been in the district she had only managed to make enemies among the members of her own class.

There was probably no girl in the graduating class, from Julia Semple and Rosa Ball, down the line, who was not glad that the girl from the Red Mill—a charity child!—was not numbered in the regular class and had no part in the graduating exercises. Nevertheless, Ruth proposed, if it were possible, to enter the Cheslow High School in the fall, and to that end she was determined to work at her books—with Miss Cramp's help—all summer.

When it came to the last day, however, and it was known that Ruth would not come back to that school again in the autumn, the smaller girls gathered about her and were really sorry that she was to go. Forced out of any part with her own grade of pupils, Ruth had taken the little ones about her and

Alice B. Emerson

played and taught them games, had told them stories on rainy days, and otherwise endeared herself to them. And now the little folk made much of her on this last day, bringing her flowers, and little presents, and clinging about her before the afternoon session began and their parents and friends came to listen to the exercises, in a way that was very pretty to behold.

Aunt Alvirah wanted to come to the closing exercises of the school; but to expect Uncle Jabez to leave the mill in business hours for any such thing as that was altogether ridiculous to contemplate. Uncle Jabez had, however, paid some small attention to Ruth in her new dress. Before she started for school that last day she went to the mill door and showed herself to the miller.

"Well, I don't see but you look as fine as the rest of 'em," he said, slowly. "And the price ain't much. You used judgment in buying, Niece Ruth. I'll say that much for ye."

This being the first word of approval the miller had ever given her, the girl appreciated it to its full value. Since he had given her the dress she had wished more than ever to become friendly with him. But he was so moody and so given up to his accounts and the hoarding of wealth, that it seemed next to impossible for the girl to get near Uncle Jabez. Besides, he had never recovered from the bitterness engendered by the loss of the cash-box. A heavy scowl rested upon his brow all the time. Sometimes he sighed and shook his head when he sat idle at the table, or on the porch in the evening; and Ruth believed he must be mourning the money which the flood was supposed to have swept away.

But although neither of the old folks at the Red Mill came to see the graduating exercises, Ruth was not exactly unhappy. The little children showing her that they liked her so well, could not fail to be a lasting pleasure to Ruth. And Helen and Tom, with their governess, Mrs. Murchiston, attended the exercises, and Helen sat with Ruth.

"And we're going to take you home; the carriage will come for us," Helen whispered in her ear.

"No," Ruth said, shaking her head, "I cannot go home with you. You know, Uncle—"

"He is an ogre," whispered Helen, with vigor.

That made Ruth smile a little, and she told Helen what Mercy Curtis called the owner of the Red Mill, and of the fancy the lame girl had taken for Uncle Jabez. "He is 'Dusty Miller' to Mercy, and I shouldn't be surprised if Uncle Jabez had her out for a day or two, if the doctor will let her come. And you mustn't call him names, I tell you. See how good he has been to me. He gave me this new dress."

"That must have hurt him awfully," said Helen, sharply. "Not but that the dress is becoming and pretty, dear. But that's the only thing he's ever given you, I warrant—and he lost your trunk!"

The Camerons insisted upon driving Ruth as far as the Red Mill, just the same. Mrs. Murchiston was a very pleasant lady, and Helen and Tom evidently thought a good deal of her.

"I should have been glad to have you for Helen's playmate this summer, my dear," said the governess to Ruth. "And I wish you were fortunate enough to be able to go with Helen this fall. You have just the characteristics in your nature to balance dear Helen's impetuosity."

Alice B. Emerson

"Oh, I wish indeed she was going to Briarwood Hall," cried Helen.

"I shall be satisfied if the way is opened for me to go to high school," Ruth declared, smiling. "Uncle has said nothing against it, and I shall begin next week walking in to Miss Cramp's to recite."

Helen asked very minutely about Ruth's plans for going to Cheslow to recite, and the very first day of the next week, when the girl of the Red Mill started for town, who should overtake her within half a mile of the mill, but Helen and her governess going to Cheslow on a shopping errand, and drawn by Tubby, the pony. Of course, there was room for Ruth in the phaeton, and Helen and Mrs. Murchiston remained in town as long as Ruth did and brought her back with them. Ruth had time to run in and see Mercy Curtis.

"I'm coming out to the Red Mill, so now!" declared the lame girl. "I asked Doctor Davison, and he says yes. And if he says so, that uncle of yours, Dusty Miller, will have to let me. Folks have to do as Doctor Davison says, you know. And your uncle—isn't he just an ugly dear? Does he look just that cross all the time? I bet he never forgives his Enemy!"

This novel reason for liking Uncle Jabez would have been amusing had there not been a serious side to it. This odd child, with her warped and twisted fancies, was to be pitied, and Ruth secretly pitied her with all her heart. But she was careful now not to show Mercy that she commiserated her condition; that way was not the way to the cripple's heart.

Nevertheless, being a little less afraid of Uncle Jabez than she once was, that very evening she mentioned Mercy's desire to him. Uncle Jabez never smiled, but it could be said that his face relaxed when she called up the memory of Sam

Curtis' crippled daughter.

"Yes; why not?" rejoined Aunt Alvirah. "Have the poor leetle creetur out here, Jabez. She'll be no bother to you. And she kin sleep with Ruthie."

"How'll she get up and down stairs?" demanded the miller, quite surprising Ruth and Aunt Alvirah by considering this phase of the matter. "You'll have to open the East bedroom, Alviry."

"Jest as you say, Jabez," answered the old woman, very meekly, but her bright eyes sparkling as she glanced aside at Ruth. "She kin roll herself in her chair in and out of that room, and onto the porch."

"I'll see Doc. Davison when he drives by to-morrer," promised Uncle Jabez, with his usual bruskness. "If he says it's all right, she can come. I'll bring her chair and her luggage out in the wagon on Saturday. The Doc. will arrange about her being brought out comfortably."

All this was so amazing that Ruth could not speak. Except when he had been angry, or at the time his cash-box was lost when the flood came down the river, she had never heard Uncle Jabez make so long a speech. Aunt Alvirah was no person with whom she could discuss this great change in the miller; and when Doctor Davison was hailed by Mr. Potter the next day and stopped at the mill for quite half an hour to confer with him, Ruth was still more amazed.

Every other day Ruth was to go to town, if it was fair. Uncle Jabez made no comment upon her absence; nor did he put himself out in the least to arrange for any means of transportation for his niece. He seldom went to Cheslow himself, save on Saturdays.

Ruth's next trip to Miss Cramp's was on a very hot day indeed. There was a glare of hot sun on the long hill and just enough fitful breeze to sift the road-dust all over her as she walked. But—and how fortunate that was!—before she had gone far the purring of a motor-car engine aroused her attention and Tom Cameron ran along beside her in his father's auto and stopped.

"Ain't I lucky?" he cried. "Get in here, Ruthie, and I'll take you to town in a jiffy."

"I'm the lucky one, I think," said Ruth, smiling in return as she slipped into the seat beside him. "And I almost believe, Tommy Cameron, that you knew I was starting for town and came along just to give me a lift."

He grinned at her. "Don't you think you're mighty important?" he teased. "Suppose I haven't anything else to think about but you girls?"

Just the same, Ruth stuck to this belief. But she had to confess that she was glad of the ride to town. It would have been very, very hot in the sun and dust.

"And it's real summer, now," she said. "It will be hot in town. I'm so glad Mercy is going to get out of it."

"What do you mean?" demanded Tom. "Is she going to be taken away?"

Ruth told him of the remarkable interest Uncle Jabez had taken in the crippled girl. Tom could scarcely have been more surprised.

"Why, the old curmudgeon has got a decent streak in him, after all; hasn't he?" he exclaimed, rather thoughtlessly.

"Don't speak that way of him, Tom," urged Ruth. "I know you've got reason for disliking him—"

"What do you mean?" demanded Tom, turning on her sharply.

"Oh, I—Well, Tom, you know I believe I could easily find the man who almost drove the team over you the night you were hurt? And you've known it all the time, and kept still about it!"

"That mean, contemptible Jasper Parloe! He's told!" gasped Tom.

"Jasper Parloe told?" repeated Ruth. "Not me."

"Then—"

"You muttered it when they carried you to the doctor's house that night. You said it was my uncle," said Ruth, quietly. "I have known it all along, and so has Parloe, I suppose. He and I were the only persons who heard what you said when you were but half conscious. You've kept still about it so as to shield Uncle, and I thank you."

Tom looked abashed; but he was angry, too. "Confound that Parloe!" he exclaimed again. "He's been bleeding me, too! Threatened to go to my father and tell about it—and Dad would have been pretty hot with your uncle, I expect."

"It was just fine of you, Tommy," Ruth said, admiringly. "But I'd let that Parloe tell anything he liked. Uncle Jabez never meant to run you down, I'm sure."

"I tell you what," said Tom. "I'll go to him myself and talk with him. Guess I can do a little bargaining on my own hook.

If I don't make him any trouble about my accident, he ought to let you and Helen be spoons again. She's just about worrying herself sick over you."

"It will come right, Tom, in the end," returned Ruth, quietly, and repeating Aunt Alvirah's favorite word of cheer. "Uncle is changed, I believe. Think of his taking so much interest in Mercy!"

"I'll see Doctor Davison," said Tom, eagerly; "and perhaps I'll bring the sick girl out on Saturday. She ought to be very comfortable in this machine. Helen would be glad to do something for her, too."

"But you don't want to make any show of doing anything for Mercy," returned Ruth, shaking her head as she got out before the station master's cottage. "There she is at the window. She'll be curious about you, I've no doubt."

She only ran in for a few moments to see Mercy before going on to Miss Cramp's.

"That's that Cameron boy," said the crippled girl, in her sharp way. "I see him and that sister of his whizzing through this street before in their car. Wish it'd blow up some day when they're showing off."

Ruth had got so now that she never showed surprise at Mercy's harsh speeches. She refused to admit that she took the lame girl seriously in her ugly moods.

"Now, you'd better not wish that, Mercy," she laughed. "Tom wants to take you out to the Red Mill on Saturday in that same automobile. Uncle Jabez is going to take the wheel chair and your baggage. You'll like riding in the car well enough."

For a moment the cripple was silent and her eyes fell before Ruth's gaze. Suddenly the guest saw that Mercy's shoulders shook and that tears were actually dropping from Mercy's eyes.

"My dear!" she cried.

"Go away!" murmured the crippled girl. "I want to be alone. I ain't never believed," she went on, with more vigor than grammar, "that I'd ever get out to your house. Is—is it really so that I can?"

"Uncle Jabez is determined you shall come. So is Doctor Davison. So am I. Everybody is helping. Why, Mercy, you'd have to come to the Red Mill on a visit now, even if you didn't want to!" cried Ruth, laughing happily.

Alice B. Emerson

CHAPTER XXIII

IN OLAKAH GLEN

And Mercy Curtis really came to the Red Mill. Perhaps it was because of Doctor Davison, for it was notorious that when the good physician set out to do a thing, or to have it done, it was accomplished.

Yet in this case it seemed as though the miller himself had as much to do with the successful outcome of the plan as anybody. He had little to say about it—or little to say at first to the crippled girl. But he saw that Aunt Alvirah and Ruth had the east bedroom ready for Mercy's occupancy before he started to town with his usual load of flour and meal on Saturday afternoon; and he was at home in good season for supper with the empty grain sacks, the fruits of his Saturday's trading, and Mercy's wheel chair in the wagon. But before he returned to the Red Mill the Camerons' big car, with Helen and Tom and the chauffeur, flashed past the Red Mill on its way to town and in a remarkably short time reappeared with Mercy sitting beside Helen in the tonneau. Doctor Davison arrived at about the same time, too, and superintended the removal of the cripple into the house.

Mercy was as excited as she could be. There was actually color in her face. She was so excited that she forgot to be snappy, and thanked them all for their kindness to her.

"Into bed you go at once, Mercy," commanded Doctor Davison; "and in the morning you may get up as early as you please—or as early as Ruth gets up." For Ruth was to sleep on the couch in the sick girl's room during her visit to the Red Mill.

The doctor drove the Camerons away then, and adjured Mercy to be quiet, leaving her to the tender nursing of Ruth and Aunt Alvirah. Mercy was in a mood to be friendly with everybody—for once. She was delighted with Aunt Alvirah. When Uncle Jabez arrived with the wheelchair she actually made him do errands for her and talked to him with a freedom that astonished both Ruth and Mrs. Alvirah Boggs.

"There! I knew you'd do it, Dusty Miller," Mercy said to the old man, tartly. "You men are all alike—just as forgetful as you can be. It's all very well to bring this old wheelchair; but where are my two sticks? Didn't they give you my canes, Dusty Miller? I assure you I have to move around a bit now and then without using this horseless carriage. I've got to have something to hobble on. I'm Goody Two-sticks, I am. You know very well that one of my legs isn't worth anything at all."

"Ha!" croaked Jabez Potter, eyeing her with his usual frown, "I didn't bring any canes; because why? There weren't any given me. They're not in the wagon."

"My! do you always frown just like that?" demanded Mercy Curtis, in a manner which would have been impertinent in any other person, but was her natural way of speaking. "You don't waste your time in smiling and smirking; do you?"

"I never saw any use in it—unless ye had something

Alice B. Emerson

perticular to smile for," admitted Mr. Potter.

"Then it won't spoil your smile if I tell you that you'll have to find me canes somewhere if I'm to help myself at all," she said.

He gravely brought two rough staffs, measured them off at just the right height for her, and spent the bulk of the evening in smoothing the rough sticks and tacking on bits of leather at the small ends of the canes in lieu of ferrules.

The east bedroom was at the end of the passage leading from the kitchen. It was right next to Uncle Jabez's own room. They all sat in the east room that evening, for its windows opened upon the wide, honeysuckle-shaded porch, and the breeze was cool. It was the beginning of many such evenings, for although Uncle Jabez sometimes retired to his bedroom where a lamp burned, and made up his cash-book and counted his money (or so Ruth supposed) not an evening went by that the miller was not, for a time at least, in the cripple's room.

He did not talk much. Indeed, if he talked to anyone more than to another it was to Ruth; but he seemed to take a quizzical interest in watching Mercy's wry faces when she was in one of her ugly moods, and in listening to her sharp speeches.

The outdoor air and sun, and the plentiful supply of fresh milk and vegetables and farm cooking, began to make another girl of Mercy before a week went over her head. She had actually some natural color, her hands became less like bird-claws, and her hollow cheeks began to fill out.

On Sunday Mr. and Mrs. Curtis drove out to see her. The Red Mill had not been so lively a place since Ruth came to it, she knew, and, she could imagine; for many a long year before. Doctor Davison was there every day. Other neighbors were continually running in to see Mercy, or to bring something for the invalid. At first, in her old, snappy, snarly way, Mercy would say:

"Old cat! just wanted to see how humpy and mean I look. Thought I was as ugly as a bullfrog, I s'pose. I know what they're after!"

But as she really began to feel better, and slept long and sweetly at night, and altogether to gain in health, she dropped such sharp speeches and had a smile when visitors came and when they left. Everybody who drove by and saw her sitting on the porch, or wheeling herself, or being wheeled by Ruth, about the paths, had something to say to her, or waved a hand at her, and Mercy Curtis began to be pleasant mannered.

She hobbled around her room more on the "two-sticks" Uncle Jabez had made for her; but she never liked to have even Ruth see her at these exercises. She certainly did get about in a very queer manner—"just like a crab with the St. Vitus dance," so she herself said.

The doctor watched her closely. He was more attentive than he had been when she was much worse off in health; and finally, after Mercy had been at the Red Mill for nearly a month, he brought a strange physician to see her. This gentleman was a great surgeon from New York, who asked Mercy a few questions, but who watched her with so intent a look that the little crippled girl was half frightened at him. He inspired confidence, however, and when he said to her, on departing: "You are going to see me again before long," Mercy was quite excited about it. She never asked a question of Doctor Davison, or of anybody else, about the strange surgeon, or his opinion of her case; but Ruth often heard her humming an odd little song (she often made up little tunes and put words to them herself) of which Ruth did not catch the burden for some days. When Mercy was singing it she mumbled the words, or dropped her voice to a whisper whenever anybody came near. But one morning Ruth was bringing the beaten egg and milk that she drank as a "pick-me-up" between breakfast and dinner, and Mercy did not hear her coming, and the odd little song came clearly to the ears of the girl of the Red Mill:

"He's going to cure me! Oh, my back and oh, my bones!

He's going to cure me! Oh, my back and oh, my bones!"

Ruth knew instantly to what the little doggerel song referred. It is true Mercy had filched Aunt Alvirah's phrase and made it her own—and it applied to the poor child as well as to the rheumatic old woman. But it was a song of joy—a song of expectation.

Ruth tried to be even more kind to Mercy after that. She was with her almost all the time. But there were occasions when Helen and Tom Cameron really made her come out with them on some little jaunt. Since Mercy's arrival at the Red Mill the Camerons had fallen into the habit of calling occasionally, and Uncle Jabez had said nothing about it. Ostensibly they called on Mercy; but it was Ruth that they came for with the pony carriage one day and took away for a visit to Olakah Glen.

This beautiful spot was not so very far away, but it called for a picnic lunch, and Tubby was quite two hours in getting them there. It was a wild hollow, with great beech trees, and a noisy stream chaffing in a rocky bed down the middle of the glen. There were some farms thereabout; but many of the farmers were no more than squatters, for a vast tract of field and forest, including the glen, belonged to an estate which had long been in the courts for settlement.

Just before leaving all signs of civilization behind, Tom had pointed out a shanty and several outbuildings on a high hillock overlooking the road, and told the girls that that was where Jasper Parloe lived, all alone.

"I came up here fishing with some of the other fellows once, and Jasper tried to drive us out of the glen. Said he owned it. Likely story! He won't trouble us to-day."

Indeed, wild as the spot was, there was little likelihood of anybody troubling the young people, for they had Reno along. This faithful creature watched over the trio most jealously and, as they were eating on the grass, he found some sudden reason to become excited. He rose up, stiffening his back, the hair rising on his neck, and a low growl issuing from his throat. The girls were a little startled, but Tom sprang up, motioned to Helen and Ruth to keep still, and ran to the angry mastiff.

"What's the matter with you, Reno?" demanded Tom, softly, but putting a restraining hand upon his collar.

Reno lurched forward, and Tom gripped the collar tightly as he was dragged directly toward a thick dump of shrubbery not many yards away.

CHAPTER XXIV

THE INITIALS

There was no sound that Tom Cameron or the girls could hear from the shrubbery; but Reno evidently knew that somebody was lurking there. And by the dog's actions Tom thought it must be somebody whom Reno disliked.

"Oh, don't leave us, Tom!" begged Helen, running behind her brother and the mastiff.

"Come on—both of you!" muttered Tom. "We'll see what this means. Stick close to me."

He had picked up a stout club; but it was in the huge and intelligent mastiff that they all put their confidence. The dog, although he snuffed now and then as though the scent that had first disturbed him still came down the wind, had ceased to growl.

They came to a path in the thicket and followed it for a few yards only, when Reno stopped and stiffened again.

"Hush!" whispered Tom, and parted the bushes with one hand, his other still clinging to the mastic's collar.

There was a tiny opening in the shrubbery. It surrounded the foot of a huge beech tree. In some past day a careless hunter had built a fire close to the trunk of this tree. It was now hollow at the base, but vines and creepers growing up the tall tree had hidden the opening.

A man was on his knees at the foot of the tree and had drawn the matted curtain of creepers aside with one hand while with the other he reached in to the full length of his arm. He had no suspicion of the presence of the young people and Reno.

Out of the hollow in the tree trunk he drew something wrapped in an old pair of overalls. He unwrapped it, still with his back to the spot where the dog and his master and the girls stood. But the three friends could see over his shoulder as he knelt on the ground, and saw plainly that the object he had withdrawn from the tree trunk was a flat black box, evidently japanned, and there was a fair-sized brass padlock which fastened it,

"Ha, ha, ha!" chuckled the man to himself, as he wrapped the box up again in the old clothes, and then thrust it hastily into the hollow tree. "Safe yet! safe yet!"

He rose up then and without even looking about him, started directly away from the glen. He plainly had no suspicion of the presence of the dog and the trio of young folks. When he was quite out of sight and sound, Tom whispered, patting Reno:

"I declare, girls! That was Jasper Parloe!"

"That mean thing!" returned his sister. "I guess he's a miser as well as a hermit; isn't he?"

"Looks like it. I've a good mind to take that thing he put in there and hide it somewhere else. He wouldn't be so sure about it's being safe then; would he?"

"No! Don't you touch his nasty things, Tom," advised Helen, turning away.

But Ruth still stared at the hidden hollow in the tree and suddenly she darted forward and knelt where Parloe had knelt.

"What are you going to do, Ruth?" demanded her chum.

"I want to see that box—I must see it!" cried the girl from the Red Mill.

"Hold on!" said Tom. "I'll get it for you. You'll get your dress dirty."

"I wouldn't touch it," cried Helen, warningly.

"I must!" gasped Ruth, greatly excited.

"It don't belong to you," quoth Helen.

"And I'm very sure it doesn't belong to Jasper Parloe," declared Ruth, earnestly.

Tom glanced at the girl from the Red Mill suddenly, and with close attention. He seemed to understand her excitement.

"Let me in there," said the youth. "I can reach it, Ruthie."

He pushed her gently, and while Ruth and Helen held aside the mass of vines the boy crawled in and reached the bundle of rags. He carefully hauled it all forth and the japanned box tumbled out of its loose wrappings.

"There it is!" grunted Tom, getting up and wiping his hands on a tuft of grass. "What do you make of it?"

Ruth had the box in her hands. Helen, looking over her shoulder, pointed to two faded letters painted on the cover of the box.

"That belongs to Jasper Parloe. His initials are on the box," she said.

"'J. P.'—that's right, I guess," muttered Tom.

It could not be gainsaid that Parloe's initials were there. Ruth stared at them for some moments in silence.

Better put it back. I don't know what he can possibly have to hide in this way," Tom said. "But we wouldn't want to get into trouble with him. He's a mean customer."

"It isn't his box!" said Ruth, quietly.

"Why isn't it?" cried Helen, in amazement.

"I never noticed the letters on the box before. The box has been cleaned since I saw it—"

"You don't mean that it is your uncle's cash-box, Ruth?" interrupted Tom, in excitement.

"Why, you ridiculous boy!" declared Helen. "You know that was lost in the flood."

"I don't know. Do you?" Tom demanded, shortly.

"But, Ruth!" gasped Helen.

"It looks like Uncle Jabez's box," Ruth whispered.

"But the letters! Jasper Parloe's initials," cried the hard-to-be-convinced Helen Cameron.

"They're uncle's initials, too," explained Ruth, quietly.

"Whew!" ejaculated Tom. "So they are. 'J. P.—Jabez Potter.' Can't get around that."

"Well, I never!" gasped Helen.

"Do you suppose all old Jabe's money is in this?" muttered Tom, weighing the cash-box in his hands. "It can't be in coin."

"I do not know that he had much money in coin," said Ruth. "I think he used to change the gold and silver for notes, quite frequently. At least, Aunt Alvirah says so."

"But suppose it should be Parloe's after all?" objected Helen.

"Let's find that out," said Tom, vigorously. "Come on, girls. We'll finish eating, pack up, and start back. We'll drive right up to Parloe's and show him this box, and ask him if it is his. If he says yes, we'll make him come along to the mill and face Mr. Potter, and then if there is any doubt of it, let them go before a magistrate and fight it out!"

The girls were impressed with the wisdom of this declaration, and all went back to rescue the remains of their luncheon from the birds and from a saucy gray squirrel that had already dropped down to the lowest limb of the tree under which they had spread their cloth, and who sat there and chattered angrily while they remained thereafter, as though he considered that he had been personally cheated out of a banquet.

The girls and Tom were so excited that they could not enjoy the remainder of the nice things that Babette had packed in their lunch basket They were soon in the carriage, and Tubby was startled out of a pleasant dream and urged up the hilly road that led through the woods to the squatter's cabin, where Jasper Parloe had taken up his quarters after he had been discharged from employment at the Red Mill.

CHAPTER XXV

ENDINGS AND BEGINNINGS

When the pony carriage drove into the little clearing about the squatter's hut, Parloe was pottering about the yard and he stood up and looked at them with arms akimbo and a growing grin upon his sly face.

"Well, well, well!" he croaked. "All together, air ye? Havin' a picnic?"

"We've been down yonder in the glen," said Tom, sternly.

For an instant Jasper Parloe changed color and looked a bit worried. But it was only for an instant. Then he grinned again and his little eyes twinkled just as though he were amused. But Tom kept on, bluntly, saying:

"We found something there, Parloe, and we came up here to see if it belongs to you."

"What's that?" asked the man, drawing nearer. "I ain't lost nothing."

"Don't say that," said Tom, quickly. "At least, don't say you haven't hidden something."

But he could not catch Mr. Parloe again. The man shook his head slowly and looked as though he hadn't the least idea of what Tom was driving at.

"Look here," continued the boy, and drew forth the japanned box.

"Well! Well!" and Jasper's mean little eyes twinkled more than ever. "You don't mean to say you found that down yonder?"

"We did," said Tom, tartly.

"Now, where was it?"

"Where it had been hidden," snapped Tom, quite disgusted with the old man. "Where it was supposed to be very safe, I reckon."

"Like enough, Tom," said Jasper, mildly. "What do you reckon on doing with it?"

"You don't claim it to be yours, then?" demanded Tom, in some surprise.

"No-o," said Parloe, slowly.

"It has your initials on it," said Helen, quickly.

"That's odd, ain't it?" returned Parloe, standing where he was and not offering to touch the box. "But other people have the same initials that I have." His grin grew to huge proportions, and he looked so sly that nothing but his high, bony nose kept his two little eyes from running together and making one eye of it. "Jabe Potter, for instance."

"Then you think this is likely to be Mr. Potter's?" queried Tom.

"Couldn't say. Jabe will probably claim it. He would take advantage of the initials, sure enough."

"And why don't you?" asked Helen.

"'Cause me and Jabe are two different men," declared Parloe, righteously. "Nobody ever could say, with proof, that Jasper Parloe took what warn't his own."

"This is my uncle's cash-box, I am very sure," interposed Ruth, with some anger. "It was not swept away the day of the flood. You were there in his little office at the very moment the waters struck the mill, and we saw you running from the place as though you were scared."

"Jefers-pelters!" croaked Jasper. "It was enough to scare anybody!"

"That may be. But you weren't too scared to grab this box when you ran. And you must have hidden it under your coat as you left the mill. I am going to tell my uncle all about it— and how we saw you down the hill yonder, looking at this very box before you thrust it back in its hiding place."

Jasper Parloe grew enraged rather than frightened by this threat.

"Tell!" he barked. "You tell what ye please. Provin's another thing. I don't know nothin' about the box. I never opened it. I don't know what's in it. And you kin tell Jabe that if he tries to make me trouble over it I'll make him trouble in a certain locality—he knows where and what about."

"I shall give him the box and tell him how it came into my possession," repeated Ruth, firmly, and then she and her friends drove away.

They hurried Tubby back to the Red Mill and Ruth ran in ahead of her friends with the cash-box in her hands. The moment Uncle Jabez saw it he started forward with a loud cry. He almost tore the box from her grasp; but then became gentle again in a moment.

"Gal!" he ejaculated, softly, "how'd ye git this away from Parloe?"

"Oh, Uncle! how did you know he had it?"

"I've been suspicious. He couldn't scarce keep it to hisself. He ain't opened it, I see."

"I don't think he has."

"We'll see. Tell me about it," urged the miller, staring at Helen and Tom as they approached.

Ruth told him all about it. She pointed, too, to the fact that Helen and Tom—and especially Tom's dog—had had more to do with the recovery of the cash-box than she had. Uncle Jabez listened and nodded as though he appreciated that fact. Meanwhile, however, he hunted up the key to the japanned box and unlocked it.

It was plain that the contents of the box were for the most part securities in the shape of stocks and bonds, with a good deal of currency in small notes. There was a little coin—gold and silver—packed into one compartment. Uncle Jabez counted it all with feverish anxiety.

"Right to a penny!" he gasped, when he had finished, and mopped the perspiration from his brow. "The rascal didn't touch it. He didn't dare!"

"But he'll dare something else, Uncle," said Ruth, hastily. "I believe he's going right to Mr. Cameron to make you trouble."

"Ah-ha!" exclaimed Uncle Jabez, and looked hard at Tom.

"I'm sorry if he makes trouble about that old thing, Mr. Potter," said Tom, stumblingly. "I've tried to keep his mouth shut—"

"Ah-ha!" said Uncle Jabez, again. Then he added: "And I shouldn't be at all surprised, young man, if you'd given Jasper money to keep his mouth shut—eh?"

Tom flushed and nodded "I didn't want any row—especially when Helen and I think so much of Ruth."

"You wouldn't have bought Jasper off for my sake, I reckon," said Jabez, sharply. "You wouldn't have done it for my sake?"

"Why should I?" returned Tom, coolly. "You never have been any too friendly towards me."

"Hah!" said the miller, nodding. "That's true. But let me tell you, young man, that I saw your father about the time I ran you down. We don't get along very well, I admit. I ain't got much use for you Camerons. But I had no intention of doing you harm. You can believe that, or not. If you will remember, the evening you went over that embankment on the Wilkins Corners road, I came up behind you. My mules were young, and your dog jumped out at them and scared them. They bolted, and I never knew till next day that you had been knocked over the embankment."

"We'll let bygones be bygones, Mr. Potter," said Tom, good-humoredly. "I came out of it all right."

"But you had no business to pay Jasper Parloe money for keeping still about it," said the miller, sourly. "Being bled by a blackmailer is never the action of a wise man. When he threatened me I went to your father at once and got ahead of Parloe. We agreed to say nothing about it—that's about all we did agree on, however," added Mr. Potter, grimly. "Now you children run along. Ruth, come here. I figger I owe you something because of the finding of this box. Yes! I know how much the others had to do with it, too. But they'd never been over there in Olakah Glen if it hadn't been for you. I'll make this up to you. I never yet owed a debt that I didn't repay in full. I'll remember this one, gal."

But so much happened in those next two weeks, following the finding of the cash-box, that Ruth quite forgot this promise on her uncle's part. She realized, however, that he seemed really desirous of being kind to her, and that much of his grimness had disappeared.

Everybody at the Red Mill—and many other people, too—had their thoughts fixed upon Mercy Curtis at this time. She had been getting stronger all the while. She had been able to hobble on her two sticks from her bedroom to the porch. She had been to ride half a dozen times in the Camerons' automobile. And then, suddenly, without other warning, Doctor Davison and the strange surgeon who had once examined Mercy, appeared in a big limousine car, with a couch arranged inside, and they whisked Mercy off to a sanitarium some miles away, where she was operated on by the famous surgeon, with Doctor Davison's help, and from which place the report came back in a few days that the operation had been successful and that Mercy Curtis would—in time—walk again!

Meanwhile, Ruth had kept up her recitations to Miss Cramp, often walking back and forth to town, but sometimes getting "a lift," and the teacher pronounced her prepared to enter the Cheslow High School. She had taken the studies that Helen Cameron had taken, and, on comparing notes, the chums found that they were in much the same condition of advancement.

"Oh, if you were only going to Briarwood with me, instead of to Cheslow High!" wailed Helen, one day, as they sat on the porch of the Red Mill house.

"Ah, dear!" said Ruth, quietly, "don't talk about it. I want to go with you more than I ever wanted to do anything in my whole life—"

"What's that?" exclaimed Uncle Jabez's gruff voice behind them. "What's that you want to do, Ruth?"

"To—to go to boarding school, Uncle," stammered his niece.

"Hah!" grunted the miller. "Ain't you calculatin' on going to high school?"

"Oh, Mr. Potter!" broke in Helen, frightened by her own temerity. "That isn't the school Ruth wants to go to. I am going to Briarwood Hall, and she wants to go, too. Do, do let her. It would be—it would be just heavenly, if she could go there, and we could be together!"

abez Potter came out upon the porch and looked down upon his niece. The grim lines of his face could not relax, it seemed; but his eyes did seem to twinkle as he said:

"And that's the greatest wish of your life; is it, Ruth?"

"I—I believe it is, Uncle Jabez," she whispered, looking at him in wonder.

"Well, well!" he said, gruffly, dropping his gaze. "Mebbe I owe it ye. My savin's of years was in that cash-box, Ruth. I—I—Well, I'll think it over and see if it can be arranged about this Briarwood business. I'll—I'll see your Aunt Alvirah."

And that Uncle Jabez Potter "saw about it" to some purpose is proven by the fact that the reader may meet Ruth and her friends again in the next volume of this series to be entitled "Ruth Fielding at Briarwood Hall; Or, Solving the Campus Mystery."

"Perhaps he isn't such an ogre after all," whispered Helen, when she and Ruth were alone.

"Not after you get to know him," replied the girl of the Red Mill, with a quiet smile.

THE END

Alice B. Emerson

Choose from Thousands of 1stWorldLibrary Classics By

A. M. Barnard
Ada Leverson
Adolphus William Ward
Aesop
Agatha Christie
Alexander Aaronsohn
Alexander Kielland
Alexandre Dumas
Alfred Gatty
Alfred Ollivant
Alice Duer Miller
Alice Turner Curtis
Alice Dunbar
Allen Chapman
Alleyne Ireland
Ambrose Bierce
Amelia E. Barr
Amory H. Bradford
Andrew Lang
Andrew McFarland Davis
Andy Adams
Angela Brazil
Anna Alice Chapin
Anna Sewell
Annie Besant
Annie Hamilton Donnell
Annie Payson Call
Annie Roe Carr
Annonaymous
Anton Chekhov
Archibald Lee Fletcher
Arnold Bennett
Arthur C. Benson
Arthur Conan Doyle
Arthur M. Winfield
Arthur Ransome
Arthur Schnitzler
Arthur Train
Atticus
B.H. Baden-Powell
B. M. Bower
B. C. Chatterjee
Baroness Emmuska Orczy
Baroness Orczy
Basil King
Bayard Taylor
Ben Macomber
Bertha Muzzy Bower
Bjornstjerne Bjornson

Booth Tarkington
Boyd Cable
Bram Stoker
C. Collodi
C. E. Orr
C. M. Ingleby
Carolyn Wells
Catherine Parr Traill
Charles A. Eastman
Charles Amory Beach
Charles Dickens
Charles Dudley Warner
Charles Farrar Browne
Charles Ives
Charles Kingsley
Charles Klein
Charles Hanson Towne
Charles Lathrop Pack
Charles Romyn Dake
Charles Whibley
Charles Willing Beale
Charlotte M. Braeme
Charlotte M. Yonge
Charlotte Perkins Stetson
Clair W. Hayes
Clarence Day Jr.
Clarence E. Mulford
Clemence Housman
Confucius
Coningsby Dawson
Cornelis DeWitt Wilcox
Cyril Burleigh
D. H. Lawrence
Daniel Defoe
David Garnett
Dinah Craik
Don Carlos Janes
Donald Keyhoe
Dorothy Kilner
Dougan Clark
Douglas Fairbanks
E. Nesbit
E. P. Roe
E. Phillips Oppenheim
E. S. Brooks
Earl Barnes
Edgar Rice Burroughs
Edith Van Dyne
Edith Wharton

Edward Everett Hale
Edward J. O'Biren
Edward S. Ellis
Edwin L. Arnold
Eleanor Atkins
Eleanor Hallowell Abbott
Eliot Gregory
Elizabeth Gaskell
Elizabeth McCracken
Elizabeth Von Arnim
Ellem Key
Emerson Hough
Emilie F. Carlen
Emily Bronte
Emily Dickinson
Enid Bagnold
Enilor Macartney Lane
Erasmus W. Jones
Ernie Howard Pie
Ethel May Dell
Ethel Turner
Ethel Watts Mumford
Eugene Sue
Eugenie Foa
Eugene Wood
Eustace Hale Ball
Evelyn Everett-green
Everard Cotes
F. H. Cheley
F. J. Cross
F. Marion Crawford
Fannie E. Newberry
Federick Austin Ogg
Ferdinand Ossendowski
Fergus Hume
Florence A. Kilpatrick
Fremont B. Deering
Francis Bacon
Francis Darwin
Frances Hodgson Burnett
Frances Parkinson Keyes
Frank Gee Patchin
Frank Harris
Frank Jewett Mather
Frank L. Packard
Frank V. Webster
Frederic Stewart Isham
Frederick Trevor Hill
Frederick Winslow Taylor

Friedrich Kerst
Friedrich Nietzsche
Fyodor Dostoyevsky
G.A. Henty
G.K. Chesterton
Gabrielle E. Jackson
Garrett P. Serviss
Gaston Leroux
George A. Warren
George Ade
Geroge Bernard Shaw
George Cary Eggleston
George Durston
George Ebers
George Eliot
George Gissing
George MacDonald
George Meredith
George Orwell
George Sylvester Viereck
George Tucker
George W. Cable
George Wharton James
Gertrude Atherton
Gordon Casserly
Grace E. King
Grace Gallatin
Grace Greenwood
Grant Allen
Guillermo A. Sherwell
Gulielma Zollinger
Gustav Flaubert
H. A. Cody
H. B. Irving
H.C. Bailey
H. G. Wells
H. H. Munro
H. Irving Hancock
H. R. Naylor
H. Rider Haggard
H. W. C. Davis
Haldeman Julius
Hall Caine
Hamilton Wright Mabie
Hans Christian Andersen
Harold Avery
Harold McGrath
Harriet Beecher Stowe
Harry Castlemon
Harry Coghill
Harry Houidini

Hayden Carruth
Helent Hunt Jackson
Helen Nicolay
Hendrik Conscience
Hendy David Thoreau
Henri Barbusse
Henrik Ibsen
Henry Adams
Henry Ford
Henry Frost
Henry James
Henry Jones Ford
Henry Seton Merriman
Henry W Longfellow
Herbert A. Giles
Herbert Carter
Herbert N. Casson
Herman Hesse
Hildegard G. Frey
Homer
Honore De Balzac
Horace B. Day
Horace Walpole
Horatio Alger Jr.
Howard Pyle
Howard R. Garis
Hugh Lofting
Hugh Walpole
Humphry Ward
Ian Maclaren
Inez Haynes Gillmore
Irving Bacheller
Isabel Cecilia Williams
Isabel Hornibrook
Israel Abrahams
Ivan Turgenev
J.G.Austin
J. Henri Fabre
J. M. Barrie
J. M. Walsh
J. Macdonald Oxley
J. R. Miller
J. S. Fletcher
J. S. Knowles
J. Storer Clouston
J. W. Duffield
Jack London
Jacob Abbott
James Allen
James Andrews
James Baldwin

James Branch Cabell
James DeMille
James Joyce
James Lane Allen
James Lane Allen
James Oliver Curwood
James Oppenheim
James Otis
James R. Driscoll
Jane Abbott
Jane Austen
Jane L. Stewart
Janet Aldridge
Jens Peter Jacobsen
Jerome K. Jerome
Jessie Graham Flower
John Buchan
John Burroughs
John Cournos
John F. Kennedy
John Gay
John Glasworthy
John Habberton
John Joy Bell
John Kendrick Bangs
John Milton
John Philip Sousa
John Taintor Foote
Jonas Lauritz Idemil Lie
Jonathan Swift
Joseph A. Altsheler
Joseph Carey
Joseph Conrad
Joseph E. Badger Jr
Joseph Hergesheimer
Joseph Jacobs
Jules Vernes
Julian Hawthrone
Julie A Lippmann
Justin Huntly McCarthy
Kakuzo Okakura
Karle Wilson Baker
Kate Chopin
Kenneth Grahame
Kenneth McGaffey
Kate Langley Bosher
Kate Langley Bosher
Katherine Cecil Thurston
Katherine Stokes
L. A. Abbot
L. T. Meade

L. Frank Baum
Latta Griswold
Laura Dent Crane
Laura Lee Hope
Laurence Housman
Lawrence Beasley
Leo Tolstoy
Leonid Andreyev
Lewis Carroll
Lewis Sperry Chafer
Lilian Bell
Lloyd Osbourne
Louis Hughes
Louis Joseph Vance
Louis Tracy
Louisa May Alcott
Lucy Fitch Perkins
Lucy Maud Montgomery
Luther Benson
Lydia Miller Middleton
Lyndon Orr
M. Corvus
M. H. Adams
Margaret E. Sangster
Margret Howth
Margaret Vandercook
Margaret W. Hungerford
Margret Penrose
Maria Edgeworth
Maria Thompson Daviess
Mariano Azuela
Marion Polk Angellotti
Mark Overton
Mark Twain
Mary Austin
Mary Catherine Crowley
Mary Cole
Mary Hastings Bradley
Mary Roberts Rinehart
Mary Rowlandson
M. Wollstonecraft Shelley
Maud Lindsay
Max Beerbohm
Myra Kelly
Nathaniel Hawthrone
Nicolo Machiavelli
O. F. Walton
Oscar Wilde

Owen Johnson
P.G. Wodehouse
Paul and Mabel Thorne
Paul G. Tomlinson
Paul Severing
Percy Brebner
Percy Keese Fitzhugh
Peter B. Kyne
Plato
Quincy Allen
R. Derby Holmes
R. L. Stevenson
R. S. Ball
Rabindranath Tagore
Rahul Alvares
Ralph Bonehill
Ralph Henry Barbour
Ralph Victor
Ralph Waldo Emmerson
Rene Descartes
Ray Cummings
Rex Beach
Rex E. Beach
Richard Harding Davis
Richard Jefferies
Richard Le Gallienne
Robert Barr
Robert Frost
Robert Gordon Anderson
Robert L. Drake
Robert Lansing
Robert Lynd
Robert Michael Ballantyne
Robert W. Chambers
Rosa Nouchette Carey
Rudyard Kipling
Saint Augustine
Samuel B. Allison
Samuel Hopkins Adams
Sarah Bernhardt
Sarah C. Hallowell
Selma Lagerlof
Sherwood Anderson
Sigmund Freud
Standish O'Grady
Stanley Weyman
Stella Benson
Stella M. Francis

Stephen Crane
Stewart Edward White
Stijn Streuvels
Swami Abhedananda
Swami Parmananda
T. S. Ackland
T. S. Arthur
The Princess Der Ling
Thomas A. Janvier
Thomas A Kempis
Thomas Anderton
Thomas Bailey Aldrich
Thomas Bulfinch
Thomas De Quincey
Thomas Dixon
Thomas H. Huxley
Thomas Hardy
Thomas More
Thornton W. Burgess
U. S. Grant
Upton Sinclair
Valentine Williams
Various Authors
Vaughan Kester
Victor Appleton
Victor G. Durham
Victoria Cross
Virginia Woolf
Wadsworth Camp
Walter Camp
Walter Scott
Washington Irving
Wilbur Lawton
Wilkie Collins
Willa Cather
Willard F. Baker
William Dean Howells
William le Queux
W. Makepeace Thackeray
William W. Walter
William Shakespeare
Winston Churchill
Yei Theodora Ozaki
Yogi Ramacharaka
Young E. Allison
Zane Grey